First World War
and Army of Occupation
War Diary
France, Belgium and Germany

1 INDIAN CAVALRY DIVISION
Lucknow Cavalry Brigade
Corps of Dragoons. 1st King's Dragoon Guards
31 August 1914 - 31 December 1916

WO95/1174/2

The Naval & Military Press Ltd
www.nmarchive.com
Published in association with The National Archives

Published by

The Naval & Military Press Ltd

Unit 10 Ridgewood Industrial Park,

Uckfield, East Sussex,

TN22 5QE England

Tel: +44 (0) 1825 749494

www.naval-military-press.com

www.nmarchive.com

This diary has been reprinted in facsimile from the original. Any imperfections are inevitably reproduced and the quality may fall short of modern type and cartographic standards.

© **Crown Copyright**
Images reproduced by permission of The National Archives, London, England, 2015.

Contents

Document type	Place/Title	Date From	Date To
Heading	WO95/1174/2		
Heading	B E F 1 Ind. Cav. Div. Lucknow Bde. 1 Kings Dragoon GDS To 1914 Aug To 1916 Dec		
Heading	War Diary of the 1st King's Dragoon Guards From 31st August To 25th December 1914		
War Diary	Lucknow	31/08/1914	08/10/1914
War Diary	Bombay	10/10/1914	16/10/1914
War Diary	At Sea	19/10/1914	20/10/1914
War Diary	Manseillers	12/11/1914	16/11/1914
War Diary	Aden	28/10/1914	28/10/1914
War Diary	Port Said	05/11/1914	05/11/1914
War Diary	Alexandrea	06/11/1914	07/11/1914
War Diary	Marseilles	17/11/1914	19/11/1914
War Diary	Orleans	22/11/1914	07/12/1914
War Diary	Lillers	21/12/1914	21/12/1914
War Diary	Norrent Fontes	23/12/1914	25/12/1914
Heading	War Diary of Kings Dragoon Guards From 9th January 1915 To 11th January 1915		
War Diary	Lusbourg	09/01/1915	09/01/1915
War Diary	Festubert	09/01/1915	11/01/1915
Map			
Heading	War Diary of 1st King's Dragoon Guards From 8th January 1915 To 19th May 1915		
War Diary	Lesboury	08/01/1915	07/03/1915
War Diary	Febvin	11/03/1915	11/03/1915
War Diary	Lapugnoy	12/03/1915	12/03/1915
War Diary	Auchel	14/03/1915	14/03/1915
War Diary	Flechin	17/03/1915	24/04/1915
War Diary	Oxalaere	28/04/1915	28/04/1915
War Diary	St Jans Ter Biezen	29/04/1915	02/05/1915
War Diary	Oxaliare	05/05/1915	05/05/1915
War Diary	Rincq	06/05/1915	17/05/1915
War Diary	Le Revillon	18/05/1915	18/05/1915
War Diary	Burbure	19/05/1915	19/05/1915
Heading	War Diary with Appendices of 1st King's Dragoon Guards. From 1st April 1915 To 30th June 1915		
War Diary	Flechin	03/04/1915	24/04/1915
War Diary	Oxelaere	28/04/1915	28/04/1915
War Diary	St. Jans-Ter-Biezen	29/04/1915	02/05/1915
War Diary	Oxelaere	05/05/1915	05/05/1915
War Diary	Rincq	06/05/1915	17/05/1915
War Diary	Le Reveillon	18/05/1915	18/05/1915
War Diary	Burbure	19/05/1915	19/05/1915
War Diary	Hooge	01/06/1915	02/06/1915
War Diary	Erkelsbrugge	06/06/1915	10/06/1915
War Diary	Vlamertinghe	12/06/1915	13/06/1915
War Diary	Erkelsbrugge	13/06/1915	15/06/1915
War Diary	Rincq	17/06/1915	17/06/1915
Diagram etc	Scale 1/5000 Appendix		

Miscellaneous	1st King's Dragoon Guards. Casualty List from 31st May to 3rd June 1915.		
Heading	War Diary with Appendices of 1st King's Dragoon Guards From 1st July 1915 To 30th September 1915		
War Diary	Rincq	03/07/1915	01/08/1915
War Diary	Matringhem	02/08/1915	02/08/1915
War Diary	Maresquel	03/08/1915	03/08/1915
War Diary	Le Plouy	04/08/1915	04/08/1915
War Diary	St Leger	04/08/1915	06/08/1915
War Diary	Halloy les Pernois	10/08/1915	22/08/1915
War Diary	Wood E of Forceville	23/08/1915	23/08/1915
War Diary	Authville	24/08/1915	02/09/1915
War Diary	E of Forceville	03/09/1915	03/09/1915
War Diary	St Gratien	04/09/1915	04/09/1915
War Diary	Halloy les Pernois	04/09/1915	04/09/1915
War Diary	St Gratien	05/09/1915	05/09/1915
War Diary	Halloy les Pernois	05/09/1915	05/09/1915
War Diary	St Gratien	06/09/1915	11/09/1915
War Diary	Halloy les Pernois	10/09/1915	11/09/1915
War Diary	St Gratien	12/09/1915	12/09/1915
War Diary	Authville	13/09/1915	16/09/1915
War Diary	St Gratien	17/09/1915	17/09/1915
War Diary	Halloy les Pernois	19/09/1915	22/09/1915
War Diary	Autheux	23/09/1915	30/09/1915
Map	R.F. 1/20000		
Heading	War Diary of 1st King's Dragoon Guards From 1st October 1915 To 31st December 1915		
War Diary	Autheux	02/10/1915	13/10/1915
War Diary	Bernaville	14/10/1915	22/10/1915
War Diary	Molliens Vidame	23/10/1915	06/11/1915
War Diary	Rincq	27/05/1915	27/05/1915
War Diary	Oxelaere	28/05/1915	28/05/1915
War Diary	Vlamertinge	31/05/1915	31/05/1915
War Diary	Molliens Vidame	08/11/1915	18/11/1915
War Diary	Longpre	22/11/1915	16/12/1915
War Diary	Le Montant	21/12/1915	31/12/1915
Heading	War Diary of 1st King's Dragoon Guards From 1st January 1916 To 31st January 1916		
War Diary	Quesnoy-Le-Montant	09/01/1916	31/01/1916
Heading	War Diary of 1st King's Dragoon Guards From 1st February To 29th February 1916		
War Diary	Quesnoy-Le-Montant	03/02/1916	22/02/1916
Heading	War Diary of 1st King's Dragoon Guards From 1st March 1916 To 31st March 1916		
War Diary	Quesnoy-Le-Montant	02/03/1916	27/03/1916
War Diary	Gueschart	31/03/1916	31/03/1916
Heading	War Diary of 1st King's Dragoon Guards From 1st April 1916 To 30th April 1916		
War Diary	Gueschart	01/04/1916	12/04/1916
War Diary	Neuf Moulin	13/04/1916	15/04/1916
War Diary	Gueschart	17/04/1916	30/04/1916
Heading	War Diary of 1st King's Dragoon Guards From 1st May 1916 To 31st May 1916		
War Diary	Gueschart	01/05/1916	01/05/1916
War Diary	St Ricquer	05/05/1916	07/05/1916
War Diary	Gueschart	10/05/1916	10/05/1916

War Diary	Sericourt	11/05/1916	30/05/1916
Heading	War Diary of 1st King's Dragoon Guards From 1st June 1916 To 30th June 1916		
Miscellaneous	To D.A.G. Ind: Sect: 3rd Echelon. G.H.Q	04/07/1916	04/07/1916
War Diary	Sericourt	01/06/1916	30/06/1916
Heading	War Diary of 1st King's Dragoon Guards From 1st July 1916 To 31st July 1916		
War Diary	Grouches	01/07/1916	01/07/1916
War Diary	Frohen Le Grand	02/07/1916	19/07/1916
War Diary	Cambligneul	20/07/1916	21/07/1916
War Diary	Neuville St Vaast	22/07/1916	28/07/1916
War Diary	Cambligneul	30/07/1916	31/07/1916
Heading	War Diary of 1st King's Dragoon Guards From 1st August 1916 To 31st August 1916		
War Diary	Cambligneul	01/08/1916	01/08/1916
War Diary	Monchy Breton	05/08/1916	09/08/1916
War Diary	Humbercourt	10/08/1916	31/08/1916
Heading	War Diary of 1st King's Dragoon Guards From 1st September 1916 To 30th September 1916		
War Diary	Humbercourt	02/09/1916	03/09/1916
War Diary	Mezerolles	04/09/1916	04/09/1916
War Diary	Canchy	05/09/1916	11/09/1916
War Diary	Frohen Le Grand	12/09/1916	12/09/1916
War Diary	Grouches	13/09/1916	13/09/1916
War Diary	Querrieux	14/09/1916	15/09/1916
War Diary	Morlancourt Camp	16/09/1916	26/09/1916
War Diary	Mametz	27/09/1916	27/09/1916
War Diary	Bussy Les Daours	28/09/1916	28/09/1916
War Diary	Hangest	29/09/1916	29/09/1916
War Diary	Vauchelles	30/09/1916	30/09/1916
Heading	War Diary of 1st King's Dragoon Guards From 1st October 1916 To 30th November 1916		
War Diary	Machy	01/10/1916	30/10/1916
Miscellaneous	Supplement To War Diary For October 1916		
War Diary	Miannay	01/11/1916	29/11/1916
Heading	War Diary of 1st King's Dragoon Guards From 1st December 1916 To 31st December 1916		
War Diary	Miannay	01/12/1916	31/12/1916

WO 95/17412

BEF

1 IND. CAV. DIV.

LUCKNOW BDE.

1 KINGS DRAGOON GDS

1914 AUG to 1916 DEC

WAR DIARY

OF THE

1ST KING'S DRAGOON GUARDS.

From 31st August to 25th December 1914.

Army Form C. 2118.

WAR DIARY
or
INTELLIGENCE SUMMARY
(Erase heading not required.)

Instructions regarding War Diaries and Intelligence Summaries are contained in F. S. Regs.; Part II. and the Staff Manual respectively. Title pages will be prepared in manuscript.

[Stamp: ADJUTANT GENERAL INDIA / 28. JAN. 1915 / BASE OFFICE]

[Stamp: No 3 Section A. G.'s Office at Base / I.E.F. "D" / S. Sec:n / Passed to _____ on 28/1/15]

Hour, Date, Place	Summary of Events and Information	Remarks and references to Appendices
31. 8.14 Lucknow	Received order to mobilize	
" 9.14 "	Mobilization completed	
23. 10.14 "	Left Bombay embarked on the _____ to take over new Mason guns at this overseas base	23 I. O. R. men were on furlough in England
	The strength of the regiment moving from Lucknow was 18 Officers. 532 men 512 horses.	
	The officers present with the regiment when mobilized was	
	Lt Col. Bell-Smyth	Lieuts. Cary-Byes
	Major Wickham	Major Wickham
	Capt. Kent	Lent ex Lucres
	Capt. Ag. Turner	Major Pakenham
	Capt. Nicholls	Capt. Gordon
	" Ferry	" Sussex
	" Cooper	Lt. Hawkins
	Lt. Fleming	" Holt
	" Alexander	
	" Goss	Attaches 7th D. Gds
	" Blackmore	2/Lt. Ames
	2/Lt. Raffles	" Richardson
	" Ward	" Graham-Holt
	" Carleton-Smith	" Kirkern
	" Card	
	Capt. & Qr Mr. Wells	

Army Form C. 2118.

Instructions regarding War Diaries and Intelligence
Summaries are contained in F.S. Regs., Part II.
and the Staff Manual respectively. Title pages
will be prepared in manuscript.

WAR DIARY
or
INTELLIGENCE SUMMARY

(Erase heading not required.)

Hour, Date, Place	Summary of Events and Information	Remarks and references to Appendices
8. 10.14 Lucknow	The regiment entrained for Bombay as follows	Left Lucknow 9.0 am & 10.14 Arr. Bombay 3 pm 10.10.14
	1st train 5 officers 179 men 159 horses	
	2nd " 8 " 190 " 184 "	3 pm 10.10.14
	3rd " 3 " 148 " 148 "	10.55 am
		The entraining & detraining arrangements at Lucknow were perfect but at Bombay the
10. 10.14 Bombay	A. & B. & C Squadron arrived went into camp on the Maidan	horses were kept on the train in great heat 2 hours before they could be embarked although the trains were all punctual.
11. 10.14 Bombay	D. Squadron & ½ C Squadron arrived	
	A. B. Squadrons embarked on H.T. Chilka	
	(Strength 6 Officers 1 Medical Officer 373 men 193 horses)	
	B & C Squadrons were ordered to embark on H.T. Franz Ferdinand	
	the same day but the ship was not ready	
12. 10.14 "	17 men & 42 horses arrived from the Innskilling Dragoons	
	to complete our first reinforcement	

Army Form C. 2118.

WAR DIARY
or
INTELLIGENCE SUMMARY

(Erase heading not required.)

Instructions regarding War Diaries and Intelligence Summaries are contained in F. S. Regs., Part II. and the Staff Manual respectively. Title pages will be prepared in manuscript.

Hour, Date, Place	Summary of Events and Information	Remarks and references to Appendices
12. 10. 14. Bombay	B. C. Squadrons & Head Quarters embarked on H.T. Varsova Ferdinand (Strength 7 Officers 213 men 198 horses)	The horse accommodation was so bad that the Bombay Ferry officer refused to take 42 horses they were embarked next day.
13. 10. 14.	Embarked on H.T. Palmacotta (11 Officers 29 men 42 horses)	
16. 10. 14.	The convoy consisting of Expeditionary Forces A. B. C. "I" troopships escorted by the "Euryalus" Duke of Edinburgh "Dalhousie" Hardinge & "Buffren" sailed from Bombay	
19. 10. 14. At Sea.	Expeditionary Force B. C. left the convoy for the Persian Gulf & "Ban Chen" respectively and the convoy was joined by the 2nd Convoy from Karachi	
20. 10. 14.	H.T. Varsova Ferdinand owing to engine troubles had to fall out of the convoy & was escorted (& finally towed on to Aden by the "Duffren" reaching Aden Harbour on the 23rd The convoy proceeded to Marseilles passing Aden on the 24th Suez on the 30th. Port Said on the 31st reached Marseilles on Nov 10th	

Army Form C. 2118.

WAR DIARY
or
INTELLIGENCE SUMMARY

(Erase heading not required.)

Instructions regarding War Diaries and Intelligence Summaries are contained in F. S. Regs., Part II. and the Staff Manual respectively. Title pages will be prepared in manuscript.

Hour, Date, Place	Summary of Events and Information	Remarks and references to Appendices
12 11 14 Marseilles	A . D Squadron disembarked & went into billets	From horses including one charger died on Hts. "A" T
18 11 14 "	C . D Squadrons entrained for Orleans & arrived there 12 midnight 19/20. Any detraining immediately & marched out to camp at Le Boheet.	Chllea, arriv'd on Hts Falmouth. The E.O.C Cavalry Division remained on the fishermen transports & the horses on arrival at Marseille
28 10 14 Aden	H T "Franz Ferdinand" having effected repairs sailed for Suez reaching there 3. 11. 14. Port Said 6. 11. 14 having passed through the canal in the record time of 11 hours. Orders were received to proceed to Alexandria & disembark there. Alexandria was reached that evening under escort of a destroyer	
5 11 14 Port Said		
6 11 14 Alexandria	D C Squadrons disembarked on the quay & orders were received to proceed immediately to Marseilles without escort	
7 11 14 Alexandria	D C re-embarked & engines worked having been completed the "Franz Ferdinand" sailed this evening. Off the west coast of Sardinia a heavy north westerly gale was encountered against which it was impossible to make headway.	

WAR DIARY or INTELLIGENCE SUMMARY

(Erase heading not required.)

Army Form C. 2118.

Instructions regarding War Diaries and Intelligence Summaries are contained in F. S. Regs., Part II. and the Staff Manual respectively. Title pages will be prepared in manuscript.

Hour, Date, Place	Summary of Events and Information	Remarks and references to Appendices
17.11.14 Marseilles	The ship was put about & a new course taken to the East of Sardinia. On emerging from the shoals of Bonifacio she was again compelled to alter the Rt to taken under the lee of the shoals of France	
19.11.14	H.T. Seang Choon arrived at Marseilles & B.C. Squadrons disembarked on the quay side on the 18th having lost only two horses. One from fever in Bombay harbour & the other from accidents	
22.11.14 Orleans.	1st Re-inforcements were sent from here to Le Havre O.C. Squadrons entrained for Orleans. B.C. Squadrons joined the Remainder of the Regiment in camp at Le Rouvres & completed the Lucknow Cavalry Brigade consisting of: H.Q.Q.: 29th Cavalry 36th Scots Horse U (Battery) R.H.A	

Army Form C. 2118.

WAR DIARY
or
INTELLIGENCE SUMMARY
(Erase heading not required.)

Instructions regarding War Diaries and Intelligence Summaries are contained in F. S. Regs., Part II. and the Staff Manual respectively. Title pages will be prepared in manuscript.

Hour, Date, Place	Summary of Events and Information	Remarks and references to Appendices
22. 11. 14 Orléans	The following officers joined the regiment at Orléans	
	Major Williams, 2nd in command.	
	Capt. C.R.A. Clegg. (A)	
	Lieut Crossley (Special Res. late R.H.A) (A)	
	2/Lt Speir (B)	
	" Richardson (B)	
	" Strahan-Holt (C)	
	" Wilson (A)	
28. 11. 14	The following officers were attached to the regiment for duty	
	Capt. P.L. Thompson (35th Scinde Horse) posted to C	
	" H.A.D. Johnson. 8 Pl Cavalry " B	
	" N.D. Remington (Res. Indian Army) " D	
7. 12. 14	On the night of 6th 7/8 the regiment entrained for Railhead (reaching Fillers on the 8th) where they detrained and marched into billets	
21. 12. 14 Fillers	The Brigade marched at 6 am went into billets as follows:-	
	R.H.Q. - H Battery at Sorans-Sonbras Light Cavalry & B Pillars	
	36th Jacobs Horse, Ham Brigade Headquarters Sorans-Sonbras	

Army Form C. 2118.

WAR DIARY
or
INTELLIGENCE SUMMARY
(Erase heading not required.)

Instructions regarding War Diaries and Intelligence Summaries are contained in F. S. Regs., Part II. and the Staff Manual respectively. Title pages will be prepared in manuscript.

Hour, Date, Place	Summary of Events and Information	Remarks and references to Appendices
23.12.14 Forrest Louks	Major General Fanshawe C.B took over command of the 1st Indian Cavalry Division which was composed of the Lucknow, Sialkot & Ambala Brigades	
25. 12.14 Forrest Louks	The 1st Division went further west into billets as follows Lucknow Brigade near Frenchin — Sialkot Brigade near Poly Ambala Brigade near Berny. The Lucknow Brigade was distributed as follows. Dragoons Headquarters & 11 Battery Frenchin & D.G. Festubury Fagot Cavalry Fontaine — Vies — Bordans and Jacobs Horse Herderin	

[signature]
Commanding 1st Division

WAR DIARY

OF

Kings Dragoon Guards.

From 9th January 1915 TO 11th January 1915.

WAR DIARY
INTELLIGENCE SUMMARY
(Erase heading not required.)

King's (Liverpool) Dragoons

Army Form C. 2118.

Hour, Date, Place	Summary of Events and Information	Remarks and references to Appendices
9.1.15 Lestrem	In accordance with orders received (Appendix A) the regiment paraded dismounted at 9.15 a.m. & marched 3 miles to Brigade's rendezvous (Appendix B) at Lestrem to meet motor buses at 11.30 a.m. After waiting & there news was brought that the buses were travelling via FONTAINE-LES-BOULOGNE being unable to leave the main road. The Regiment marched thither & met the buses half way. At 1.15 (the men were aboard the 14 buses (one & two being provided for the horses) proceeded to PALFART where the Brigade convoy of no less was formed. The whole moved off at 2.0 p.m. for BETHUNE reached there at 5.0 p.m. Two A.T. carts picked up the half casts & A.T. carts carrying rations & entrenching tools which had been sent on ahead. (App. C)	Strength Officers Warrant Officers Other Ranks 25 14 320
9.1.15 Festubert	The Brigade marches to FESTUBERT the men carrying their blankets & waterproof sheets & entrenching tools. A.T. carts accompanied the Brigade carrying rations & machines. The regiment reached the station at FESTUBERT village at 6.45 p.m. & took over from the Sialkot Brigade. The A.T. carts were off loaded & returned to Brigade H.Q. to draw the next day's rations they assisted in procuring 220 sets men of the 17th Lancers & the 17th Lancers	

Army Form C. 2118.

WAR DIARY
or
INTELLIGENCE SUMMARY
(Erase heading not required.)

Instructions regarding War Diaries and Intelligence Summaries are contained in F. S. Regs., Part II. and the Staff Manual respectively. Title pages will be prepared in manuscript.

Hour, Date, Place	Summary of Events and Information	Remarks and references to Appendices
9.1.15 Festubert	were not fully relieved until midnight owing to the communication trenches being flooded & the difficulty of getting sick & wounded from the trenches. The regiment occupied the two firing line trenches with B Squadron (75 men & 1 maxim) on the right & two troops A Squadron on the left. Sir reorganising two troops of A held the supporting trenches. C & D Squadrons were in reserve in the village of Festubert with orders to hold the reserve trenches on the outskirts of the village in case of the advanced trenches being evacuated. Two men hours his goods into the trenches & two of them belonged to the team were thoroughly & were shot by the Indian Cavalry whilst passing in rear of their lines. No further casualties occurred during the night. The enemy kept up the usual shell continuously & maintained a sharp fire on the advanced trenches. Regimental trans Quarters & the whole village were actively sniped all night. Our wounded were all evacuated during the night.	
10.1.15 Festubert	At 4.0 am C Squadron relieved the 2 troops of A in the firing line trenches. During the day the Engineers cooperated with an attack	

Army Form C. 2118.

WAR DIARY
INTELLIGENCE SUMMARY

(Erase heading not required.)

Instructions regarding War Diaries and Intelligence Summaries are contained in F. S. Regs., Part II. and the Staff Manual respectively. Title pages will be prepared in manuscript.

Hour, Date, Place	Summary of Events and Information	Remarks and references to Appendices
10.1.15 Festubert	Relieved by the 2nd Infantry Brigade in accordance with orders received (Appendix D). Desultory rifle fire heard all day, interrupted by bursts from us in co-operation with the attack. There were no casualties. The water in the trenches rose appreciably being about the waist in most places.	
10.1.15	At 5.0.p.m. "B" Squadron were relieved by "D" after doing 24 hours in the firing line. The two troops "C" in left firing trench were relieved by two troops "A" and let's two troops of "A" who had done 24 hours in the support trenches were relieved by two troops "B". "B" Squadron was very exhausted from exposure practically no effective from that moment. During this night reports were received from both his trenches that the's weak if had risen a foot & was now up to the mens armpits. Many men were already very exhausted. Sick men were ordered to be sent out of the trenches but these could not be replaced as there were no fresh men to send into the trenches.	
11.1.15	At 4.0.a.m. orders were received from Brigade Head Quarters to return from the 1st two trenches on the supporting	

Army Form C. 2118.

WAR DIARY
or
INTELLIGENCE SUMMARY
(Erase heading not required.)

Hour, Date, Place	Summary of Events and Information	Remarks and references to Appendices
11.1.15 Festubert Trenches	As the personnel of the table 2 was increased to 30 men each of the reporters the total of which men available, a double company of 4th Gurkha Rifles Brothers was sent up from reserve to be in reserve under the orders of O.C. 1st B.B.G's. The usual sniping went on during the day. Our reference there was very little firing. The enemy did not occupy our forward lines trenches & wanted they taking (their own front line holding). This accuracy of the sniping last day might found to first offers firing largely used. Only two casualties occurred during this relief. Revictualisation of food & drink.	
11.1.15 Festubert	At 5.30 p.m. a Maxim was sent up to the left support trench in order to strengthen the se-entrant caused by the retirement from the front line trenches. Very little firing took place during the day. Our listening posts a direct at 10.30 a.m. & during daytime shelled Lattecure in rear of FESTUBERT & the E end of the village during the afternoon. In accordance with orders for relief (Appendix E) the 7thBos Brigade arrived at 6.10 a.m. to relieve the Jardine Brigade	

WAR DIARY
or
INTELLIGENCE SUMMARY

Army Form C. 2118.

(Erase heading not required.)

Instructions regarding War Diaries and Intelligence Summaries are contained in F. S. Regs., Part II. and the Staff Manual respectively. Title pages will be prepared in manuscript.

N° 3 Section
A. G's Office at Base
I. E. Force
Passed to _____ S. Sect.n
on _____

Hour, Date, Place	Summary of Events and Information	Remarks and references to Appendices
11.15. February.	On the arrival of the snowstorms O.B.B Squadrons moved off to Bethune and the Carts so such were evacuated by the Bearer Sec.n Field Ambulance. The remainder by Reg.tl Bearers – 97 cases of the snowstorms. As tea by food were explained to the snowstorms who two troops of C/ Squadron maxim went reserves by the two troops snowstorms – Maxim. The completion of such was reported to Brigade Headquarters at 6.15 p.m. The Regiment assembled at Bethune at 10.0 p.m. Motor buses were awaiting arrival 1.0 a.m. the Brigade left for its billets. The Regiment reached Lestrem at 8.0 a.m.	Forces. Evacuated cases 21 Cases on returning to billets from exposure, frostbite 50 exposure, frostbite.

J.Willoughby Lieut Col
Commanding R.H.G

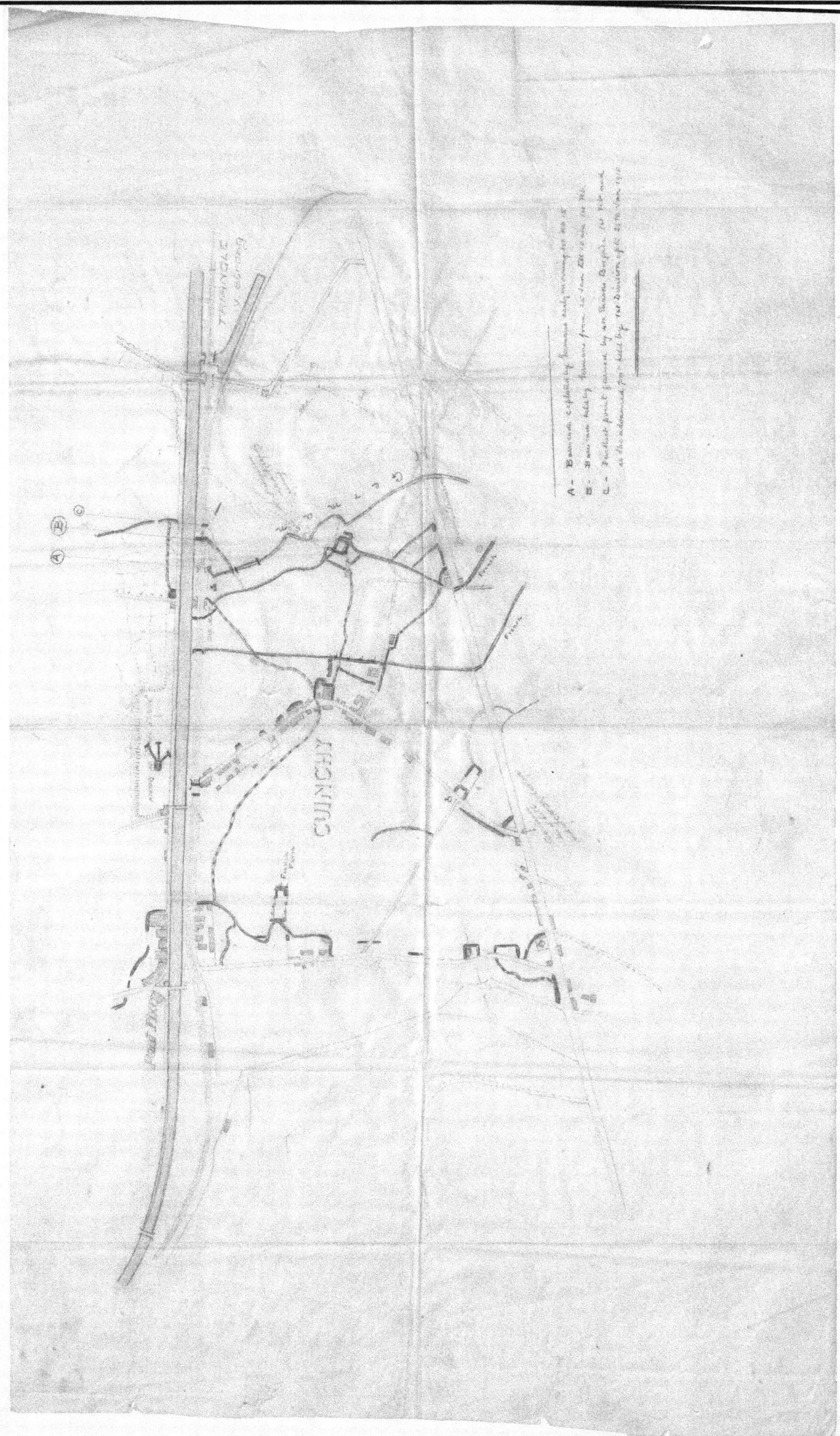

Serial No. 71.

121/5501 Robinson

WAR DIARY
OF
1st King's Dragoon Guards.
From 8th February 1915 to 19th May 1915.

WAR DIARY or INTELLIGENCE SUMMARY

Army Form C. 2118.

Hour, Date, Place	Summary of Events and Information	Remarks and references to Appendices
Testbury 8. 1. 15.	2/Lt Murray Johnson - 2/Lt Hoggett 45 & 200 men & 19 horses moved from Base	
28. 1. 13.	18 & M Jacques - 18 Q N B Harding 93 retired one tie	
13. 2. 15.	2/Lieut. R Burton (Temp. Commission) joined from Base	
2/Lieut Farmington		
26. 2. 15.	1 & O & 208 men joined from Base	
2. 3. 15.	On the 2nd 3rd 9th & March 13 Officers + 200 men marched at 5.30 am to FONTAINE LES- HERMANS & proceeded thence by motor bus and dug into tent trenches near B. Renard returning to Willets each evening	
1. 3. 15.	The regiment marched at 6.30am to Brigade close Willets at Lebon.	
Febr. 11. 3. 15.	The regiment marched at 2.30 am to NEDONCHELLE and thence by a zigzag of readiness in the BOIS de DAMES	

Army Form C. 2118.

WAR DIARY
or
INTELLIGENCE SUMMARY

(Erase heading not required.)

Instructions regarding War Diaries and Intelligence Summaries are contained in F. S. Regs., Part II. and the Staff Manual respectively. Title pages will be prepared in manuscript.

Place	Hour, Date	Summary of Events and Information	Remarks and references to Appendices
LAPOGNOY	12.3.15	Near LAPOGNOY and bivouacked three during the attack at NEUVE CHAPELLE.	
AUCHEL	14.3.15	Marched at noon to close billets at AUCHEL.	
	15.3.15	Marched at midnight to FLECHIN and went into billets there at 8.0 am. The regiment was billeted as follows H.Q. Maxim C.+D. Squadrons at FLECHIN A Squadron in OUHEM. B Squadron in BONCOURT	
FLECHIN	17.3.15	Lieut Thompson R.V.D. took over veterinary charge of the regiment.	
FLECHIN	20.3.15	11 charges arrived.	
	22.3.15	Capt Thompson + Capt Johnson transferred to sick. Second + sick horses respectively.	
	24.3.15	2/Lt Benton transferred to the Reserve Regt from next leave	
	28.3.15	Major Hunt resumed took over command of B Squadron	
	29.3.15	Capt Benton - - - - C -	
	30.3.15	Lt Gladstone transferred to 1st Res Regt from next leave	

1247 W 3299 200,000 (E) 8/14 J.B.C. & A. Forms/C. 2118/11.

Army Form C. 2118.

WAR DIARY
or
INTELLIGENCE SUMMARY

(Erase heading not required.)

Instructions regarding War Diaries and Intelligence Summaries are contained in F. S. Regs., Part II. and the Staff Manual respectively. Title pages will be prepared in manuscript.

Hour, Date, Place			Summary of Events and Information	Remarks and references to Appendices
Hazebrouck	3	4	15	28 horses arrived from Bess.	
—	3	4	15	On the 3rd ult. OTR 12 Officers + 200 men proceeded by motor bus to ROBECQUE + constructed two lines trenches returning each evening to billets.	
—	24	4	15	The regiment marched at 7.15 pm to Brigade rendezvous at ESTREE BLANCHE thence Regiments marched in order 29th 36th R.D.F. via MORBECQUE - RODUSTOIRE - HAZEBROUCK - EBBLINGHEM - STAPLE to QUEUE of OXELAERE where the regiment went into close billets at 3.0 am	
OXELAERE	28	4	15	Marched at 12.15 pm via CASSEL and STEENVOORDE to ST JAN STER BIEZEN + went into billets west of the village	
ST JAN STER BIEZEN	29	4	15	Remained at instant readiness to move.	
	30	4	15		
	1	5	15		

Army Form C. 2118.

WAR DIARY
or
INTELLIGENCE SUMMARY

(Erase heading not required.)

Instructions regarding War Diaries and Intelligence Summaries are contained in F. S. Regs., Part II. and the Staff Manual respectively. Title pages will be prepared in manuscript.

Hour, Date, Place		Summary of Events and Information	Remarks and references to Appendices
27 JAN STEENVOORDE	4.5.15	Marched at 6 am via WATOU back to original billets at OXELAERE arrived at 10.0 am	
OXELAERE	5.5.15	Marched at 2 am to billets at RINCQ reaching there at 7 am. The regiment was billeted as follows HQ Maxim MG in RINCQ. A B C E Squadrons in FLEMING HEM D MARNE & LA JUMELLE	
RINCQ	6.5.15	A. Squadron marched at 9.0 am to LESTREM to be attached to Indian Corps for patrol duty.	
"	7.5.15	18 horses joined from Base.	
"	8.5.15	The A. Carts forming the A. Echelon of the regiment were returned to Base Transport Officers for disposal complete and replaced by 5 limbered G.S. wagons each with a team of four mules in rods & chains with men of the regiment as drivers, previously trained at advanced Horse depot. Brought 20 teams 1 NCO in charge 20 mules.	

WAR DIARY
or
INTELLIGENCE SUMMARY

(Erase heading not required.)

Army Form C. 2118.

Hour, Date, Place	Summary of Events and Information	Remarks and references to Appendices
RINCQ 13.5.15	19 horses arrived from Base	
RINCQ 17.5.13	Marched at 4.30pm to position of readiness at LE BEVILLON near Allouagne went into close billets at 8.30pm	
LE BEVILLON 18.5.13	Marched at 2pm to close billets at BURBURE in orders to get the men under cover	
BURBURE 19.5.13	Marched at 1.10pm to my original billets at RINCQ to make room for 4th Division. During this move B Echelon did not accompany the regiment but remained parked at MAMETZ	

14.5.15.

WAR DIARY

With Appendices.

1st. King's Dragoon Guards.

From 1st April 1915 to 30th June 1915.

Army Form C. 2118.

WAR DIARY
or
INTELLIGENCE SUMMARY
(Erase heading not required.)

Instructions regarding War Diaries and Intelligence Summaries are contained in F. S. Regs., Part II. and the Staff Manual respectively. Title pages will be prepared in manuscript.

Hour, Date, Place	Summary of Events and Information	Remarks and references to Appendices
FLECHIN 3.4.15.	21 horses arrived from base.	The average weight carried by the horse is roughly 20 stones, as follows:-
". 3.4.15.	On the 3rd, 4th and 5th, 12 officers and 200 men proceeded by Motor bus to ROBECQUE and constructed 3rd line trenches, returning each evening to billets in FLECHIN.	Man, complete kit, rifle, lance bandolier (90 rds) bayonet 194 lbs.
" 21.4.15 23.4.15	12 officers and 200 men proceeded by Motor bus to ROBECQUE and constructed 3rd line trenches, returning each evening to billets in FLECHIN.	Saddle. British Warm Mackintosh. Straps. Shoe case (2 shoes) Peg. Pad. Sword. Shackle. Horse bandolier (30 rds) Corn sack filled. 2 blankets. Headgear.
" 24. 28.4.15	The regiment marched at 7.15 a.m. to a Brigade rendezvous at ESTREE BLANCHE; thence Brigade marched via MAMETZ-ROQUETOIRE WARDRECQUES-EBLINGHAM-STAPLE to QUE d'OXELLAERE where the regiment went into close billets at 3 p.m. Marched at 12.15 p.m. via CASSEL and STEENVOORDE to ST.JANS-TER-BIEZEN and went into close billets W. of that village.	82 lbs.
OXELAERE 28.4.15		
ST.JANS-TER-BIEZEN 29.4.15 30.4.15 1.5.15	Remained at instant readiness to move.	19 stones 10 lbs.
2.5.15.	WATOU Marched at 6 a.m. via WATOU and CASSEL back to original billets at OXELAERE and arrived at 10 a.m.	
OXELAERE 5.5.15.	Marched at 2 a.m. to billets at RINCQ reaching there at 7 a.m. Regiment was billeted as follows; H.Q., Maxim Gun, and "B" Sqdn. in RINCQ, "A" Sqdn. GLOMENGHEM, "D" Sqdn WARNE, "C" Sqdn. LA JUNELLE.	

Army Form C. 2118.

WAR DIARY
INTELLIGENCE SUMMARY
(Erase heading not required.)

Instructions regarding War Diaries and Intelligence Summaries are contained in F. S. Regs., Part II. and the Staff Manual respectively. Title pages will be prepared in manuscript.

Hour, Date, Place	Summary of Events and Information	Remarks and references to Appendices
RINCQ 6.5.15	"A" Sqdn marched at 9 a.m. to LESTREM to be attached to Indian Corps, 1st Army, for patrol duty.	
" 10.5.15	18 horses arrived from Base.	
" 15.5.15	19 horses arrived from Base.	
" "	The A.T.Carts mules and personnel forming A echelon were returned to Divisional Transport officer for disposal, and the regiment received 5 limbered G.S.Wagons, each with 4 mules in ride and drive. Drivers were men of the regiment previously trained at Advanced Horse Transport Depot, strength 1 N.C.O., 10 men, 20 mules.	
" 16.5.15 " 17.5.15	The regiment was put under two hours to move. The regiment marched at 4.30 p.m. to Brigade rendezvous near AIRE and thence to a position of readiness at LE REVEILLON near BETHUNE and went into close billets at 8.30 p.m.	
LE REVEILLON 18.5.15	Marched at 2 p.m. to close billets at BURBURE in order to get the men under cover.	
BURBURE 19.5.15	The whole of the 1st Indian Cavalry Division returned to their original billeting area, to make room for the 7th Division which was being relieved from the trenches. The regiment marched at 1.45 p.m. to RINCQ. During this move to LE REVEILLON, A Echelon alone accompanied the regiment, spare pack saddles being taken at the rate of 1 per troop and 2 for H.Q and Max.Gun. Men were to be dismounted to provide horses to carry the packs, but in the event of an opportunity arising for the cavalry to break through, practically 4 days rations would be carried with the regiment thus:- Iron ration and unconsumed portion of previous day's	

1247 W 3299 200,000 (E) 8/14 J.B.C. & A. Forms/C. 2118/11.

Army Form C. 2118.

WAR DIARY
INTELLIGENCE SUMMARY

(Erase heading not required.)

Instructions regarding War Diaries and Intelligence Summaries are contained in F. S. Regs., Part II. and the Staff Manual respectively. Title pages will be prepared in manuscript.

Hour, Date, Place	Summary of Events and Information	Remarks and references to Appendices
HOOGE 1.6.15	reconnitring of the 3rd Dragoon Guards reported that there were no Germans in the Chateau buildings and these were occupied pending the arrival of the regiment. On the arrival of the regiment about 11 pm. the 3rd Dragoon Guard posts were relieved and work was commenced by A, C & D sqdns with borrowed tools, but was greatly delayed owing to the late arrival of the pioneers and regimental tools: B Squadron was employed in carrying up rations and R.E.Stores. A Echelon under Capt. Wells, brought up the rations each night to the "dumping ground" in ZOUAVE WOOD, where ration parties met it. The road was invariably shelled each night by the Germans.	
" 2.6.15	By daylight works A. B. & C were partially dug and D & E. commenced. Work A. was occupied by D. Sqdn; work B. by A. Sqdn; and work C. by two troops of C. Sqdn: At 2.45 a.m. B.Sqdn; and two troops C. were withdrawn to ZOUAVE WOOD and troops were ordered to complete the existing works as best they could by daylight. There was a shortage of sandbags and pickets. At 5 a.m. the enemy commenced shelling the buildings in HOOGE and our trenches with H.E and ceased at 8.30 a.m. There was intermittant shelling during the day being especially heavy between 2 p.m. and 4 p.m. That night the existing works were improved, works D & E. were completed and a splinter proof at F. The windows of the Chateau and stables were sandbagged and loopholed and the pioneers wired a portion of the front towards the lake, under cover of covering parties of 15 men each to the N. and E. At dawn the Chateau and annexe were each occupied by one troop C. Sqn. under Capt. Cooper, and B. Sqdn., and B. Sqdn relieved D Sqdn in work A. D Sqdn was then withdrawn to ZOUAVE WOOD. Very severe shelling commenced at 5 a.m. with H.E. Shrapnel and "MINEWERFER" on the Chateau buildings and all trenches and continued until 12.40 p.m. All the men were	The casualties during the first 24 hours were; 1 officer.} 7 men. } wounded.

WAR DIARY
INTELLIGENCE SUMMARY

(Erase heading not required.)

Army Form C. 2118.

Hour, Date, Place	Summary of Events and Information	Remarks and references to Appendices
HOOGE 2.6.15	withdrawn into the annexe cellar from the Chateau, those in A to cellars in the fort, leaving small observation posts. At about 1xxx&xxxxx 1 p.m. the C.O. sent D.Sqdn up in support. During the lull the works and Chateau were re-occupied and dug out where blown in. At 2 p.m. severe shelling recommenced, works A. B. & C. were blown in in many places, the machine gun at C. was buried and only two walls of the Chateau and stables remained standing. At 5 p.m. the bombardment ceased and the Germans attacked from the N. and E. Left Section. Two squadrons K.D.G's occupied the fort and buildings of HOOGE N. of the MENIN Road. The Maxim obtained a good target on 30 or 40 Germans at 300 yards and after-wards succeeded in driving in various working parties near the lake. Snipers posted in the roofs of the fort buildings also had good targets. One Squadron was then put into work A. to clear the damage done by shell fire and reoccupy the trench. Later they co-operated with xx a counter attack from the right section, on the stables, which had been occupied by the Germans. Shortly after mid-night these two squadrons and the machine gun section were relieved by one company of the Lincoln regiment and withdrew to ZOUAVE WOOD. Right Section. As soon as the shelling ceased the remains of works B. and C. were manned and the maxim unearthed and b and brought to G, but had been damaged by bombardment. The attack from the East was driven back and at dusk trench C was blocked, listening posts put out, and the remainder of the two troops holding it were withdrawn to work B. Mean-while the Germans had, on cessation of the bombardment, advanced against the annexe under cover of the Chateau. Capt. Cooper who was wounded, and the three men that remained, @m who	@ two of these were wounded.

Army Form C. 2118.

WAR DIARY
INTELLIGENCE SUMMARY

(Erase heading not required.)

Instructions regarding War Diaries and Intelligence
Summaries are contained in F. S. Regs., Part II.
and the Staff Manual respectively. Title pages
will be prepared in manuscript.

Hour, Date, Place	Summary of Events and Information	Remarks and references to Appendices
	were the survivors of two troops and were bombed out, through the stable, on to work B. They were followed up by the Germans under cover of the darkness, who then occupied the stables. They were immediately counter attacked by a part of A. Sqdn under Capt. Cheape and the stable reoccupied by post. A bombing party was applied for to counter attack the Chateau, theses did not arrive and A. and C. Sqdns were relieved by the Lincoln regiment, and withdrew to ZOUAVE WOOD, whence the regiment marched back via YPRES to huts at VLAMERTINGHE	Complete list of casualties attached. The majority occurred during the attack, losses from shell fire being comparatively small.
ERKELSBRUGGE. 6.6.15	28 N.C.O's and men arrived from base.	
" 10.6.15	Lt. Fox, Lt. Gladstone, & 2/Lt. Brown & 3 servants arrived from Base.	
VLAMERTINGHE 12.6.15.	At 8 a.m. the Germans shelled the road near the huts for about an hour with 5" high velocity Naval gun from a S.E. direction. The men were ordered to turn out of the huts and bivouac in the fields S.E. of the road.	
" 13.6.15.	They returned to the huts in the morning but as the huts were again shelled from 5 a.m. to 6 a.m. from a N.E. direction, the whole division bivouacked in fields away from the road.	
ERKELSBRUGGE 13.6.15.	1 W.O., 35 N.C.O's and men joined from Base. 13 horses arrived.	
" 14.6.15.	The regiment proceeded by bus at 6 a.m. from BRANDHOOK to billets at ERKELSBRUGGE reaching there at midday. A. Echelon marched at 5 a.m. to billets S.E. of CASSEL and rejoined the regiment the following day at RINCQ.	

Army Form C. 2118.

WAR DIARY
INTELLIGENCE SUMMARY
(Erase heading not required.)

Instructions regarding War Diaries and Intelligence Summaries are contained in F. S. Regs., Part II. and the Staff Manual respectively. Title pages will be prepared in manuscript.

Hour, Date, Place	Summary of Events and Information	Remarks and references to Appendices
ERKELSBRUGGE 15.6.15	The Brigade marched at 8 a.m. back to its own billeting area and the regiment occupied its previous billets in and round RINCQ.	The classification of the horses of the regiment, including chargers, is, at this date, English. Walers. Country Bred. 205. 93. 287.
RINCQ 17.6.15	12 riding horses arrived from base.	

1247 W 3299 200,000 (E) 8/14 J.B.C. & A. Forms/C. 2118/11.

Bellewarde
Farm

ETANG
BELLEWARDE

40
35
40

Fort
Annexe F
Château
A D E
B stable
C

Dug out

3rd DG

R.H.G.

Zouave
Wood

Dumping
Ground
for rations

Scale 1/5000 approx

1ST KING'S DRAGOON GUARDS.

Casualty List from 31st May to 3rd June 1915.

Officers killed.

    Captain W.G.F.Renton.

Officers wounded.

    Major R.S.Hunt.
    Capt: E.R.F.Cooper.
    Capt: L.W.Alexander.
    Capt: R.H.Dickson. R.A.M.C.
    Lieut: D.L.J.Carleton Smith.
    2/Lt: F.H.Murray Johnson.

N.C.O's and men killed.

No:	Rank	Name	Sdn:	Remarks.
7477	Pte:	Whiteman.S.	A	
5776	"	Peverill.J.	A	
6102	"	Hunt.W.	A	
2864	"	Adams.C.W.	A	
4087	L/C.	Atkinson.S.	A	
7383	Pte:	Bishop.E.	A	
4638	Sgt:	Cook.G.	B	
6062	Pte:	Marshall.P.	B	
3780	Sgt:	Peake.J.	C	
5887	Cpl:	Rawlings.A.S.	C	
5638	Pte:	Bowers.H.	C	
4751	Pte:	Staniland.W.	C	
75??	"	Clancey.C.E.	C	
6910	"	Walker.A.	C	
6074	L/C:	King.C.	C	
796	Pte:	Hatcher.F.G.	C	
????	"	Lindley.W.	D	
8???	"	McClay.	D	
6854	Pte	Francis	A	...... Regt: Hqtrs:
6300	Sgt:	Agombar.	B	...... Max: Gun.
8561	Pte:	Sore.E.	A	Hqtrs: (Previously rptd: missing)
5418	Sgt:	Trudgett.J.	C	" " " "

N.C.O's and men wounded.

No:	Rank	Name	Sdn:
5900	L/C:	Connell.J.H.	A
5336	"	Jones.L.	A
4069	"	Pottinger.W.	A
5888	Sgt:	Addison.J.	A
11905	Pte:	Allen.J.	A
5771	"	Bryant.E.	A
687	L/Sgt:	Fawcett.S.	A
587	L/C:	Studd.B.	A
5474	Pte:	Harrison.E.	
3824	"	Ramage.C.	A
4363	"	Ratcliffe.J.	A
7526	"	Palmer.A.	A
4467	"	Fairclough.T.	B
7386	"	Jones.W.	B
19205	"	Sinclair.A.	B
6649	"	Tanner.W.	B
19268	"	McGuire.	C
4537	Sgt:	Westoby.W.	C
6261	Cpl:	Watson.G.	C

N.C.O's and men wounded (cont:)

No:	Rank	Name	Sdn:	Remarks.
4267	Sgt:	Beech.H.	C	
6137	L/C:	Ashton.W.	C	
1878	"	Mecklenburgh.J.	C	
5532	"	Barger.H.	D	
9232	Pte:	Sydenham.H.	D	
6127	"	Timmey.E.	D	
5975	"	Drew.C.	D	
6960	Sgt:	Alford.R.	D	
4790	Pte:	Hogg.R.	D	
3821	"	Harbour.J.	D	
11990	"	Stevenson.J.	D	
5118	R.S.M.	Brewer.J.	A	.... Regt: Hqtrs:
577	L/C:	Pelling.W.	D	.... " "
3744	"	Cressey.W.	D	.... Max: Gun.
1257	"	Carpenter.W.	A	
9046	Pte:	Melloy.H.	B	
388	"	Wren.J.	B	
5301	"	Lenton.S.	A	
1984	"	Andrews.W.	C	
6590	L/C:	Smith.H.C.	C	.... (Previously reported missing)
7711	Pte:	Sullivan.D.	B	.... " " "
157	Sgt:	Melhuish.	A	
5877	L/C:	Pronson.	D	
6809	Pte:	Simpson.	D	
5531	L/C:	Simmons.	B	.... " " "

Men, died of wounds.

11670	Pte:	Chapman.A.	A	
3465	"	Pearce.J.	C	
335	"	Gower.G.	C	
3204	"	Rawson.B.	A	.... (Previously reported missing)

N.C.O's and men missing.

908	S.S.M.	Pain.W.	A	.... (Believed killed)
19154	Pte:	Murray.G.	B	" "
7524	"	Little.G.	B	" "
6293	L/C:	Kinsey.H.	C	" "
7696	Pte:	Prosser.V.	C	" "
4773	"	Overall.J.	C	" "
3536	"	Fitspatrick.	C	" "

M/.

Serial No 25

121/7286

WAR DIARY
with appendices.

OF

1st King's Dragoon Guards.

From 1st July 1915 TO 30th September 1915

Army Form C. 2118.

WAR DIARY
or
INTELLIGENCE SUMMARY

(Erase heading not required.)

Instructions regarding War Diaries and Intelligence Summaries are contained in F. S. Regs., Part II. and the Staff Manual respectively. Title pages will be prepared in manuscript.

1/3

Hour, Date, Place		Summary of Events and Information	Remarks and references to Appendices
RINCQ.	3.7.15.	Lieut: F.W.F.Card, & 40 N.C.Os: and men arrived from the Base. 6 horses arrived from the Base.	
RINCQ.	4.7.15.	1 N.C.O. arrived from the Base.	
RINCQ.	7.7.15.	5 Officers, 309 W.Os, N.C.Os and men embussed at MAMETZ at 8.0.a.m. and proceeded to LA GORGE where they went into billets; working daily digging trenches and returning to RINCQ on the evening of 11.7.15	
RINCQ.	9.7.15.	10 horses transferred to The Mobile Vety: Section.	
RINCQ.	10.7.15.	2 men arrived from the Base.	
RINCQ.	17.7.15.	5 Officers, 159 W.Os, N.C.Os: and men embussed at MAMETZ at 8.0.a.m. and proceeded to LA FOSSE where they went into billets; working in day and night shifts digging trenches.	
RINCQ.	17.7.15	5 N.C.Os: and men proceeded to join the Railhead Remount Section Indian Cavalry Corps.	
RINCQ.	19.7.15.	1 Officer 10 N.C.Os: and men embussed at MAMETZ at 8.0.a.m. and proceeded to FOSSE to join the above party. Both parties returned to RINCQ on 7.7.15.	
RINCQ.	20.7.15.	2 Men proceeded to join the Railhead Remount Section, Indian Cavalry Corps.	
RINCQ.	21.7.15.	Major: A.M.Turner assumed the duties of Brigade Major to Lucknow Cavalry Brigade. 3 men and 5 horses transferred to Lucknow Cavalry Brigade.	
RINCQ.	26.7.15.	8 horses transferred to the Mobile Veterinary Section.	

Army Form C. 2118.

WAR DIARY
or
INTELLIGENCE SUMMARY

(Erase heading not required.)

Instructions regarding War Diaries and Intelligence Summaries are contained in F.S. Regs., Part II. and the Staff Manual respectively. Title pages will be prepared in manuscript.

Hour, Date, Place	Summary of Events and Information	Remarks and references to Appendices
RINCQ. 27.7.15.	6 Remounts arrived from Base.	
RINCQ. 30.7.15.	2 Horses transferred to The Mobile Veterinary Section.	
RINCQ. 1.8.15.	The Regiment marched at 10.30.a.m. to the Brigade rendezvous at BASSE-BOULOGNE: thence the Brigade marched via BOMY to a billeting area about FRUGES. The Regiment MATRINGHEM at 2.45.p.m. and went into billets.	
MATRINGHEM. 2.8.15.	The Regiment marched at 8.0.a.m. to the Brigade rendezvous: thence the Brigade marched via COUPELLE-NEUVE-BOIS de SAIN-SAINS les FRESSIN PAPILLON-Pt112 BUISSON de PIERREPONT to CONTES to a billeting area about AUBIN ST VAST. The Regiment reached MARESQUEL at 12 noon, and went into billets.	
MARESQUEL. 3.8.15.	The Brigade marched at 9.0.a.m. via LAMBUS-DOMPIERRE-WADICOURT-BRANLINCOURT FM:-NOYELLE en CHAUSSE-YVRENCH-DOMQUEUR to a billeting area south of ABBEVILLE-BERMAVILLE Road. The Regiment went into billets at 3.0.p.m. A & B Sqdns: in DOMQUEUR, C & D Sqdns: Maxim Gun and Regtl: Hd: Qtrs: at LE PLOUY.	
LE PLOUY. 4.8.15.	The Brigade marched at 11.0.a.m. via FRANQUEVILLE-DOMART en PONTHIEU to a billeting area about ST LEGER, where the Regiment went into billets at 2.0.p.m.	
ST LEGER. 4.8.15.	Capt: & Adjt: W.R.F.Cooper rejoined Regiment from England.	
ST LEGER. 6.8.15.	The Regiment marched at 1.0.p.m. to a new billeting area, and went into billets at 2.0.p.m. as follows:- A.B.C.Sqdns: at PERNOIS. D Sqdn: M.Gun & Hd: Qtrs: at HALLOY les PERNOIS.	
HALLOY les PERNOIS. 10.8.15.	13 N.C.Os: and men, and 20 horses arrived from the Base.	

Army Form C. 2118.

WAR DIARY
or
INTELLIGENCE SUMMARY.
(Erase heading not required.)

Instructions regarding War Diaries and Intelligence Summaries are contained in F. S. Regs., Part II. and the Staff Manual respectively. Title pages will be prepared in manuscript.

Place	Date	Hour	Summary of Events and Information	Remarks and references to Appendices
HALLOY-les-PERNOIS.	15.8.15.		10 N.C.Os: and men, and 18 horses arrived from the Base.	
HALLOY-les-PERNOIS.	22.8.15.		The regiment marched from HALLOY-les-PERNOIS at 3.15.p.m. to Brigade rendezvous at WAGNIERS. (13 Officers 300 rifles 1 Asst: Surgeon 6 stretcher bearers for the trenches and 88 mounted horse holders.) The Brigade then marched via TALMAS-RUBEMPRE to BEAUCOURT (about 12 miles) arriving at 6.45.p.m. Lines were put down and the horses watered and fed. The Brigade continued the march at 8.15.p.m. (leaving the Lines down) to a wood about 1½ miles East of FORCEVILLE arriving at 11.0.p.m. The trench party bivouacked in the wood, and the horseholders and led horses of the brigade returned to BEAUCOURT under Major Harbord, 30th Lancers, with orders to remain there the following day (August 23rd) and march at night back to permanent billets. The "A" echelon of the Brigade marched at 3.0.p.m. from CANAPLES via BEAUCOURT to the wood at FORCEVILLE where it parked. The Quartermaster, 1 Officer and 27 horse holders were sent on lorries from Brigade Hd: Qtrs: The Quartermaster was left at BEAUCOURT to arrange for rations and forage for the led horse party; the remainder proceeded to the wood East of FORCEVILLE to await the arrival of the Regiment, previous to the arrival of the Regiment the wood was reconnoitred by the officers and 5 N.C.Os for suitable bivouacs for the Regiment; In addition to the above party 20 horse holders were sent up on two G.S. wagons with "A" Echelon.	
Wood E of FORCEVILLE.	23.8.15.		At 10.0.a.m. 4 Officers proceeded to AUTHUILLE to arrange for the relief with the 6th ENNISKILLING DRAGOONS. At 3.0.p.m. "B" Sqdn: marched under a guide via MARTINSART to take over a detached post 600 yards N.W. of AUTHUILLE (MacMahon's Post, also known as MOUND KEEP) relieving "C" Sqdn: 6th Dgns: at 5.0.p.m. The Maxim Guns of the Regiment paraded at 3.0.p.m. under the Brigade Machine Gun Officer and marched to MARTINSART and thence to MacMahon's Post where they relieved the gun detachments of the 6th Dgns: about 5.30.p.m	

Army Form C. 2118.

WAR DIARY
or
INTELLIGENCE SUMMARY.
(Erase heading not required.)

Instructions regarding War Diaries and Intelligence Summaries are contained in F.S. Regs., Part II. and the Staff Manual respectively. Title pages will be prepared in manuscript.

Place	Date	Hour	Summary of Events and Information	Remarks and references to Appendices
AUTHUILLE	24.8.15.		"A" "C" "D" Sqdns: and Regtl: Hd: Qtrs: and 12 pack mules carrying entrenching tools, cooking utensils, medical stores, and signalling equipment paraded at Brigade rendezvous at 7.45.p.m. the Brigade then marched via MARTINSART to AUTHUILLE and the regiment relieved 3 Sqdns: and Regtl: Hd: Qtrs: of the 6th Dgns: in the support trenches. The Officers W.Os. N.C.O's and men were quartered in splinter-proof dug-outs. Orders were issued that in case of attack "A" and "C" Sqdns: would man the portion of the perimeter Trenches E. of AUTHUILLE in support. "D" Sqdn: and Regtl: Hd: Qtrs: would fall in, in the square near the KEEP in readiness to reinforce the front line if required; later orders issued were that Regtl: Hd: Qtrs: and "D" Sqdn: would fall in in the Perimeter (The Trench S.W. of AUTHUILLE Church and await orders, the change of orders being made owing to the possibility of heavy shelling of the village if the enemy attacked. "B" Sqdn: and the machine guns would hold MacMahons Post and cover our retirement in case of retreat. The Pack mules returned to MARTINSART where they remained with 2 G.S.wagons from "A" Echelon. The G.S.Wagons formed a ration train working daily between MARTINSART and the refilling point at HEADVILLE. At MARTINSART the rations were devided up into troops and placed in bags provided for the purpose. The 12 pack mules then carried the rations into AUTHUILLE at night. "A" echelon was ordered to march to VADENCOURT on August 24th, park, and await orders.	
AUTHUILLE.	25.8.15.		The regiment supplied two working parties of 1 officer and 60 men, 1st Relief worked from 10.0.a.m. to 2.0.p.m., and the 2nd from 2.0.p.m. to 6.0.p.m. They were employed at cutting and bundling wood for revetments etc: 4 Sentry posts were provided from Regiment daily. 8 shells were dropped into the villiage by the enemy during the day A working party of 1 officer and 60 N.C.Os. and men "C" Sqdn: and 20	

Army Form C. 2118.

WAR DIARY

(Erase heading not required.)

Place	Date	Hour	Summary of Events and Information	Remarks and references to Appendices
AUTHUILLE	25.8.15.		The officers who accompanied the Regiment to the trenches were:- Major. H.J.Williams. in command. " R.S.Hunt. 2/ " " Capt: & Adjt: W.R.F.Cooper. " E.A.Wienholt. Machine Gun Officer. 2/Lt: L.Farthing. Bombing Officer. A Sqdn: Capt: A.A.Crossley. 2/Lt: A.Brown. B Sqdn: Capt: S.E.Harvey. 2/Lt: W.H.Muir. C Sqdn: Capt: R.S.Spurrier. Lt: T.H.Gladstone. D Sqdn: Capt: H.M.Fleming. Lt: A.B.Richardson. men of "A" Sqdn: were employed from 8.0.a.m. to 12 noon improving Support fire trenches S.W. of the village, this party was relieved by 1 officer and 60 men "D" Sqdn: and 20 men "A" Sqdn: who worked from 12 noon to 4.0.p.m. A few shells fell round the village furing the day.	
AUTHUILLE.	26.8.15.		2 digging parties of 1 officer and 80 men worked from 7.30.a.m. to 11.30.a.m. and 11.30.a.m. to 3.30.p.m. on the KEEP and the inner defences of AUTHUILLE. A working party of 1 N.C.O. and 14 men from "A" and "D" Sqdns: were detailed for work at 8.30.p.m. under the Divisional Signalling officer, this party finished the work in an hour and a half under the estimated time and were congratulated by the Officer i/c. "B" Sqdn: sent out a reconnoitring patrol at night to search for a supposed sniper who was suspected of lying up in the Marshes behind the AUTHUILLE LINES, no signs of a sniper were discovered. The usual amount of shelling by the enemy took place during the day.	
AUTHUILLE.	27.8.15.		The working hours of the digging parties were as follows:- 1 officer and 80 N.C.Os. and men worked from 7.30.a.m. till 11.30.a.m. and again from 3.30.p.m. to 7.30.p.m., a second party strength the same as the first party, worked from 11.30.a.m. to 3.30.p.m. and from 8.0.p.m. to 12 midnight The parties working by day were employed on the KEEP and trenches S.W. of AUTHUILLE, and the night party on the Support trenches E. of AUTHUILLE. 4 shells were burst over "C" Sqdn's working party about 12.30.p.m. no casualties. During the day a total of 34 shells were reported as having burst over the village. 1 man of the Maxim Gun was wounded in the arm by a stray bullet about 8.30.p.m. near MOUND KEEP.	
AUTHUILLE.	28.8.15.		Two digging parties worked as usual, the 1st: party working two reliefs of 4 hours each and the 2nd party 4 hours. The Maxim Guns were brought into action and ranged by "Indirect fire"	

Army Form C. 2118.

WAR DIARY
or
INTELLIGENCE SUMMARY.
(Erase heading not required.)

Remarks and references to Appendices:

Officers who accompanied Regiment to trenches. (cont)
  Lt: Col: J.A.Bell-Smyth took over command of G.Reserve Sector on the afternoon of 29th August 1915.
  2/Lt:A.Jacques & 2/Lt:T.H.Chalmers relieved Lt:T.H.Gladston & Lt:A.B.Richardson on 30th August 1915
  Major R.S.Hunt. was evacuated sick on the 2nd Sept: 1915.
  Lt: T.H.Holroyd took over medical charge of the Lucknow Cavalry Brigade 30th August 1915.

Place	Date	Hour	Summary of Events and Information
AUTHUILLE	29.8.15.		on to a mound which the enemy had been making in front of the 8th Hussars Fire trench. Lieuts: Muir and Farthing reconnoitred the various crossings over the Marsh from E. to W., North of AUTHUILLE, N.W. of our lines. Orders were issued that, to facilitate reliefs etc; the nomenclature of dismounted cavalry in the trenches will in future be as follows.— The Division..........3 dismounted brigades. The Brigade..........3 dismounted regiments. The Regiment..........4 dismounted sqdns; and so on. A large number of shells were burst over the village frequently during the day.
AUTHUILLE	30.8.15.		Working parties as on the 28th inst: Our artillery bombarded the enemy's earthworks in front of the 8th Hussars trenches at 10.0.a.m. and the Maxim Guns were kept in readiness should the enemy attempt to rebuild it. 1 man of "A" Sqdn: was injured whilst working in the KEEP through a heavy beam falling on his head, he was taken to hospital unconscious. The village was shelled at intervals as usual.
AUTHUILLE	31.8.15.		Working parties as usual. One party working on the trenches E. of the village was shelled during the afternoon. No casualties. Two officers arrived from "B" Echelon and relieved two officers from "D" and "C" Sqdns:
AUTHUILLE	1.9.15.		Working parties were provided of the usual strength, these worked for the usual hours. The daily round of shelling. No casualties. Working parties as usual. 3 Officers of the 7th Dragoon Guards arrived to arrange for the relief of the regiment on 2nd Sept: Nothing unusual occured.

Instructions regarding War Diaries and Intelligence Summaries are contained in F. S. Regs, Part II. and the Staff Manual respectively. Title pages will be prepared in manuscript.

1577 Wt.W10791/1773 500,000 1/15 D.D.&L. A.D.S.S./Forms/C. 2118.

Army Form C. 2118.

WAR DIARY
or
~~INTELLIGENCE SUMMARY~~

(Erase heading not required.)

Instructions regarding War Diaries and Intelligence Summaries are contained in F. S. Regs., Part II. and the Staff Manual respectively. Title pages will be prepared in manuscript.

Place	Date	Hour	Summary of Events and Information	Remarks and references to Appendices
AUTHUILLE	2.9.15.		Whilst Regtl: Hd: Qtrs: "A" "C" & "D" Sqdns: were in occupation of support trenches at AUTHUILLE, "B" Sqdn: and the Maxim Guns were holding a detached entrenchment known as MOUND KEEP. From this post a good view of THIEPVAL Chateau and a considerable stretch of German trenches can be obtained from a house above the Railway arch, here one of the Maxim Gun emplacements was built. The post skirted the east side of the railway line at a point where the Cavalry Division's sector overlapped the sector of the 4th Infantry Division. Here some old French trenches had been taken over which were found to be very narrow and shallow, and the traverses in a good many places were not even bullet proof. "B" Sqdn: working parties (during the occupation of the post) deepened and widened the trenches and improved the traverses, and also finished the wire entanglements in front of the position. This work had been commenced by the Enniskilling Dragoons. There were three good dug-outs in the position, but the Sqdn: started and completed a fourth one. The Sqdn: found 4 permanent posts, 2 traffic controlposts, and 2 observation posts to prevent snipers working their way down into the marshes of AUTHUILLE Wood. Maxim Gun working parties constructed alternative gun emplacements and started on 2 fresh ones, and also a new H.E. proof dug-out, these were not completed before relief. Only 3 shells fell into the post during our occupation, but the post was swept by many stray bullets at night. One G.S. wagon had been brought down to the HAMEL-AVELUY Road about ½ mile W. of AUTHUILLE at 6.0.a.m. and during the day all the entrenching tools, cooking utensils, signallers equipment, and Maxim Gun packs were loaded on the wagon, and the waggon moved off under the Brigade Transport Officer after dusk to MARTINSART. The bridge near the Quarter Guard was heavily shelled by the enemy about 12.30.p.m. and at 5.0.p.m. 4 shells were dropped over Regtl: Hd: Qtrs: just missing the new bridge over the ANCRE river. The Maxim Guns were relieved at 11.0.a.m. at MARTINSART, and the guns and ammunition boxes were carried back by men to MARTINSART, and there loaded on wagons. The	

Army Form C. 2118.

WAR DIARY
or
INTELLIGENCE SUMMARY.

(Erase heading not required.)

Instructions regarding War Diaries and Intelligence Summaries are contained in F. S. Regs., Part II. and the Staff Manual respectively. Title pages will be prepared in manuscript.

Place	Date	Hour	Summary of Events and Information	Remarks and references to Appendices
E of FORCEVILLE.	3.9.15.		detachment then marched to the Brigade rendezvous to await the arrival of the Regiment. "A" "B" "C" & "D" Sqdns: were relieved by the 7th Dragoons about 12 midnight. Regtl: Hd: Qtrs: and the Guards were relieved at 2.0.a.m. Sqdns: marched independently via MARTINSART to a point about 1½ miles E. of FORCEVILLE where 4 officers 140 N.C.Os and men and 420 led horses were awaiting the arrival of the regiment: this party had marched from permanent billets at 4.0.p.m. on the 1st: Sept:. The 2 G.S.Wagons and 12 pack mules rejoined the regiment at this point. 40 N.C.Os and men returned to permanent billets on motor lorries.	
ST GRATIEN.	4.9.15.		The Brigade marched at 4.15.a.m. to a billetting area around ST: GRATIEN-FRECHENCOURT. The Regt: arrived at ST. GRATIEN at 7.0.a.m. and 8 officers 304 N.C.Os. and men with 308 horses went into billets for the purpose of providing two working parties daily of 1 officer and 75 men each for work on the second line of defence near SENLIS the parties riding to the working area and returning on completion of shift. Working hours 1st relief, 9.0.a.m. to 12 noon, 2nd relief, 1.0.p.m. to 4.0.p.m. The remainder of the regiment and pack mules marched at 3.0.p.m. to permanent billets at HALLOY les PERNOIS arriving after a very wet march at 5.30.p.m.	
HALLOY les PERNOIS.	4.9.15.		The working parties commenced digging operations on the 2nd line of defence, riding about 10 miles to work. A echelon returned to permanent billets from VADENCOURT at 6.30.p.m.	
ST GRATIEN.	5.9.15.		Working parties employed as before on 2nd line of defence.	
HALLOY LES PERNOIS.	5.9.15.		2/Lieut: Langford. 1 man and 3 chargers joined the regiment from Base.	
ST GRATIEN	6.9.15.		5 Officers, 152 N.C.OS. and men and 156 horses marched at 8.0.p.m. back to permanent billets arriving at HALLOY les PERNOIS at 11.30.p.m. 3 officers 152 N.C.OS and men with 152 horses remained in billets	

Army Form C. 2118

WAR DIARY
or
INTELLIGENCE SUMMARY
(Erase heading not required.)

Instructions regarding War Diaries and Intelligence Summaries are contained in F.S. Regs., Part II. and the Staff Manual respectively. Title Pages will be prepared in manuscript.

Place	Date	Hour	Summary of Events and Information	Remarks and references to Appendices
ST GRATIEN	7.9.15 to 11.9.15.		at ST GRATIEN to provide a working party daily near SENLIS.	
			A working party of 1 officer and 111 N.C.Os. and men rode daily to SENLIS working on the line of defence from 9.0.a.m. to 1.0.p.m. returning to billets on completion of days work.	
HALLOY les PERNOIS	10.9.15.		Lieut: A.B.Richardson proceeded to the 1st Ind: Cavy: Divn: as A.D.C. to the G.O.C.	
HALLOY les PERNOIS.	11.9.15.		The regiment paraded at 7.15.p.m. and marched to the Brigade rendezvous at the cross roads E of WARGNIES. The Brigade under command of Lt: Col: J.A.Bell-Smyth marched at 8.0.p.m. via TALMAS-PIERREGOT-MOLLIENS AU BOIS TO the Brigade billeting area ST GRATIEN-FRENCHENCOURT arriving at 11.0.p.m. The Regiment went into the billets occupied by the digging party.	
ST GRATIEN.	12.9.15.		The Regiment, strength 14 officers 240 rifles for the trenches, and 1 man to 2 led horses, accompanied by 2 G.S.wagons and 16 pack mules, paraded at 6.0.pm and marched to the Brigade rendezvous, MONTIGNY. The Brigade marched at 7.0.pm to MARTINSART. The led horses of the Brigade returned to BEAUCOURT under the command of Lt:Col:J.A.Bell-Smyth, where they were watered and fed, and thence proceeded to permanent billets via the route they came. (40 dismounted men (for the trenches) proceeded in 2 lorries at 2.0.p.m. from Regtl: Hd: Qtrs: to point 97 East of FORCEVILLE and then marched at 7.0.p.m. on foot to MARTINSART and there awaited the arrival of the mounted men from St: GRATIEN. The Regiment then proceeded dismounted to AUTHUILLE arriving at 12 mdnt: and took over the support trenches, the relief being carried out in a similar manner to the relief of the night of the 2/3rd Sept: "B" Sqdn: occupied MacMahons Post. A.C.& D Sqdns: with the maching guns forming a reserve at AUTHUILLE ready to carry out a counter attack if necessary. 1 Sergt: 2Cpls: and 14 men were found for guards and control posts on various entrances to the village.	
AUTHUILLE	13.9.15.		Two working parties of 1 Officer and 80 N.C.Os. and men were supplied for	

Army Form C. 2118.

WAR DIARY
or
INTELLIGENCE SUMMARY
(Erase heading not required.)

Place	Date	Hour	Summary of Events and Information	Remarks and references to Appendices

			The officers who accompanied the Regiment to the trenches were.-
			     Major H.J.Williams. in command.
			     Capt: & Adjt: W.R.F.Cooper.
			     Lieut: B.M.Ward. M.Gun Officer.
			     2/Lt: L.Farthing. Bombing Officer.
			 A Sqdn: Capt: G.R.H.Cheape. 2/Lt: W.Langford.
			 B Sqdn: Capt: S.E.Harvey 2/Lt: J.L.Waggett.
			 C Sqdn: Capt: R.S.Spurrier. 2/Lt: B.Gratton-Holt.
			 D Sqdn: Lieut: H.S.Hatfield. Lieut: C.E.Wilson.
			     2/Lt: A.Brown. Staff Officer. G 1 Sub Sector.
			     Capt: E.A.Wienholt relieved Lt: B.M.Ward on 15th Sept: 1915. Lt: Ward relieved Capt: S.E.Harvey, in command of B Sqdn: 15th Sept: 1915.	

AUTHUILLE.	14.9.15.		improving the defences. These worked in two reliefs, 1st relief working from 10.0.a.m. to 2.0.p.m. and the 2nd relief from 2.0.p.m. to 6.0.p.m. Nothing unusual occurred during the day.
			
			 A working party of 1 officer and 150 men paraded under an R.E. officer at 7.30.a.m. and worked until 11.0.a.m.
			     At 1.0.p.m. the Regiment commenced to take over a portion of the front line trenches known as G.1. Sub-sector, relieving the 8th Hussars in the following manner.
			     5 N.C.Os. and 25 men of B Sqdn: 8th Hussars relieved B Sqdns: guards at MacMahons Post.
			     At 1.15.p.m. C Sqdns: Guards (1 Sgt: 2 Cpls: & 14 men) in AUTHUILLE were relieved by guards of the 8th Hussars.
			     At 2.0.p.m. D Sqdn: relieved D Sqdn: 8th Hussars.
			     At 2.15.p.m. the Officers Messess and Sqdn: cooks changed places. When the reliefs were completed the dispositions of the regiment were as follows.-
			     C Sqdn: and 2 troops of A Sqdn: and the Maxim Guns in the front line trenches with 2 troops of A Sqdn: in immediate support.
			     B & D Sqdns: occupied trenches immediately in rear and formed a local reserve to the whole of the brigade.
			     About 6.0.p.m. 1 man of B Sqdn: who was drawing water in AUTHUILLE was hit in the leg by a shrapnell bullet.
			     At 6.0.p.m. a listening post in our front line reported that the enemy were digging at a mound in their trenches.
			     At 9.15.p.m. 18 H.E.shrapnel shells burst just behind C Sqdns: trenches.	

AUTHUILLE.	15.9.15.		The enemy sent over 3 rifle grenades about 12.15.a.m. these dropped behind C Sqdns: trench, and 2 grenades were pitched over A Sqdn: No damage. A Sqdn: reported that they thought they had located a MINENWERFER in the enemy's front line trench about 100 yds: north of the Mound.	

WAR DIARY or INTELLIGENCE SUMMARY.

(Erase heading not required.)

Army Form C. 2118.

Place	Date	Hour	Summary of Events and Information	Remarks and references to Appendices
AUTHUILLE.	16.9.15.		At 2.55.p.m. 2 MINENWERFER shells pitched just over the N. of C Sqdn: trench, and at 3.5.p.m. 1 Rifle grenade landed in the same place. At 5.15.p.m. a H.E. shell hit the NORTHERN traverse in C Sqdns: trench. At 6.25.p.m. 4 more MINENWERFER shells landed in the same place as the former ones, and at 10.50.p.m. 12 rifles grenades were dropped in the wireentanglements opposite C Sqdn: No casualties occured in the Regiment. About 100 H.E. shells were dropped into AUTHUILLE during the day. At 1.30.a.m. 5 trench mortar shells were fired at the left of C Sqdns: trench. A patrol of 2 men from A Sqdn: went out twice during the night, and reconnoitred to within 30 yards of the enemy's wire entanglements: they reported that they could hear GERMAN voices and digging going on. At noon the maxim guns were relieved by those of the 153rd Infantry Brigad A.B.C. & D. Sqdns: and Regtl: Hd: Qtrs: were relieved by the GORDONS at 10.0.p.m. and marched via MARTINSART to FORCEVILLE Wood where the led horses of the regiment were waiting. The Regiment mounted and rode to ST GRATIEN arriving at 4.0.a.m. 17th Sept: 1915	
ST GRATIEN.	17.9.15.		The Regiment rested during the day, paraded at 6.0.p.m. and marched to Permanent billets, arriving at HALLOY les PERNOIS at 9.15.p.m.	
HALLOY les PERNOIS.	19.9.15.		5 N.C.Os. and men joined from the Base.	

Army Form C. 2118

WAR DIARY
or
INTELLIGENCE SUMMARY

(Erase heading not required.)

Instructions regarding War Diaries and Intelligence Summaries are contained in F.S. Regs., Part II. and the Staff Manual respectively. Title Pages will be prepared in manuscript.

Place	Date	Hour	Summary of Events and Information	Remarks and references to Appendices
HALLOY les PERNOIS.	21.9.15.		The Regiment paraded at 8.10.a.m. and marched to the Divisional rendezvous at a point 1½ miles N.W. of ST OUEN. The 1st Indian Cavalry Division paraded at 11.0.a.m. in "Line of Masses" S.E. of LA HAIE, where Field Marshall Lord Kitchener inspected the Division at 12.30.p.m.	
HALLOY les PERNOIS.	22.9.15.		The Regiment with A & B echelons paraded at 1.0.p.m. and marched to the Brigade rendezvous at the N. exit of MONTRELET. The Brigade marched at 2.0.p.m. to a billeting area about HARDINVAL. The Regiment went into close billets at 3.15.p.m. in AUTHEUX.	
AUTHEUX	23.9.15.		The Regiment remained in readiness to move.	
AUTHEUX	24.9.15.		The Regiment remained in immediate readiness to move. The Regimnt was equipped with 4 Vickers Machine Guns, the new complement for a Cavalry Regiment. The two old Maxim Guns were returned to Ordnance.	⋕ Owing to increased complement of Machine Guns 1 extra G.S. Wagon was issued to Regt: This was taken over by C Sqdn: whose limber wagon was handed over to the M.Gun detachment.
AUTHEUX	25.9.15.		The Regiment stood to, ready to move at half-an-hour's notice. The Regiments kits, and 2nd blankets were off loaded and dumped in AUTHEUX Chateau at 3.0.p.m. and the 5 G.S.wagons, under Lt: R.G.Fox proceeded to Railhead where they loaded two days rations and forage and then parked, under the orders of the Brigade Transport Officer, on the AUXILEHATEAU-DOULLENS main road, head of the column just West of RISQUETOUT facing E, and there awaited orders. At 5.0.p.m. orders were recvd: Hd: Qtrs: with ration sacks, and 1 horse holder, and 1 loader per animal, to the Reserve Supply Park at 6.0.p.m. and 2 each M.Gun and Regtl: Hd: Qtrs: with ration sacks, and 1 horse The party proceeded under 2/Lt: L.Farthing, and drew 2 days iron rations for the Regiment; returning to billets at 8.0.p.m. ⋕ 1 G.S. wagon and 4 light draught horses taken over from A.S.C. park.	
AUTHEUX	26.9.15.		The Regiment remained in immediate readiness to move on receipt of orders until 4.0.p.m., when orders were received to stand to at 2½ hours notice.	

Army Form C. 2118

WAR DIARY
or
INTELLIGENCE SUMMARY
(Erase heading not required.)

Instructions regarding War Diaries and Intelligence Summaries are contained in F.S. Regs., Part II. and the Staff Manual respectively. Title Pages will be prepared in manuscript.

Place	Date	Hour	Summary of Events and Information	Remarks and references to Appendices
AUTHEUX.	27/28.9.15.		28 N.C.Os. and men and 8 horses arrived from the Base.	
AUTHEUX.	29.9.15.		Remained in readiness at 2½ hours notice. 22 horses and 2 mules arrived from Base.	
AUTHEUX.	30.9.15.		Remained in readiness at 2½ hours notice.	Roll of officers serving with Regiment 30.9.15. Regt: Hd: Qtrs: Lt: Col: J.A.Bell-Smyth. Major H.J.Williams. Capt: & Adjt: W.R.F.Cooper. Capt: E.A.Wienholt. Capt: & Q.M. W.T.Wells. Capt: T.H.Holroyd. R.A.M.C. A Sqdn: Capt: G.R.H.Cheape. Capt: A.A.Crossley. Lieut: F.W.F.Card. 2/Lt: A.Brown. 2/Lt: W.Langford. B Sqdn: Capt: S.E.Harvey. Lieut: B.M.Ward. Lieut: W.H.Muir. 2/Lt: J.L.B.Waggett. 2/Lt: L.Farthing. C Sqdn: Capt: R.S.Spurrier. Lieut: T.H.Gladstone. Lieut: B.Gratton-Holt. 2/Lt: A.Jacques. D Sqdn: Capt: H.M.Fleming. Lieut: R.G.Fox. Lieut: H.S.Hatfield. Lieut: C.E.Wilson. 2/Lt: T.H.Chalmers.

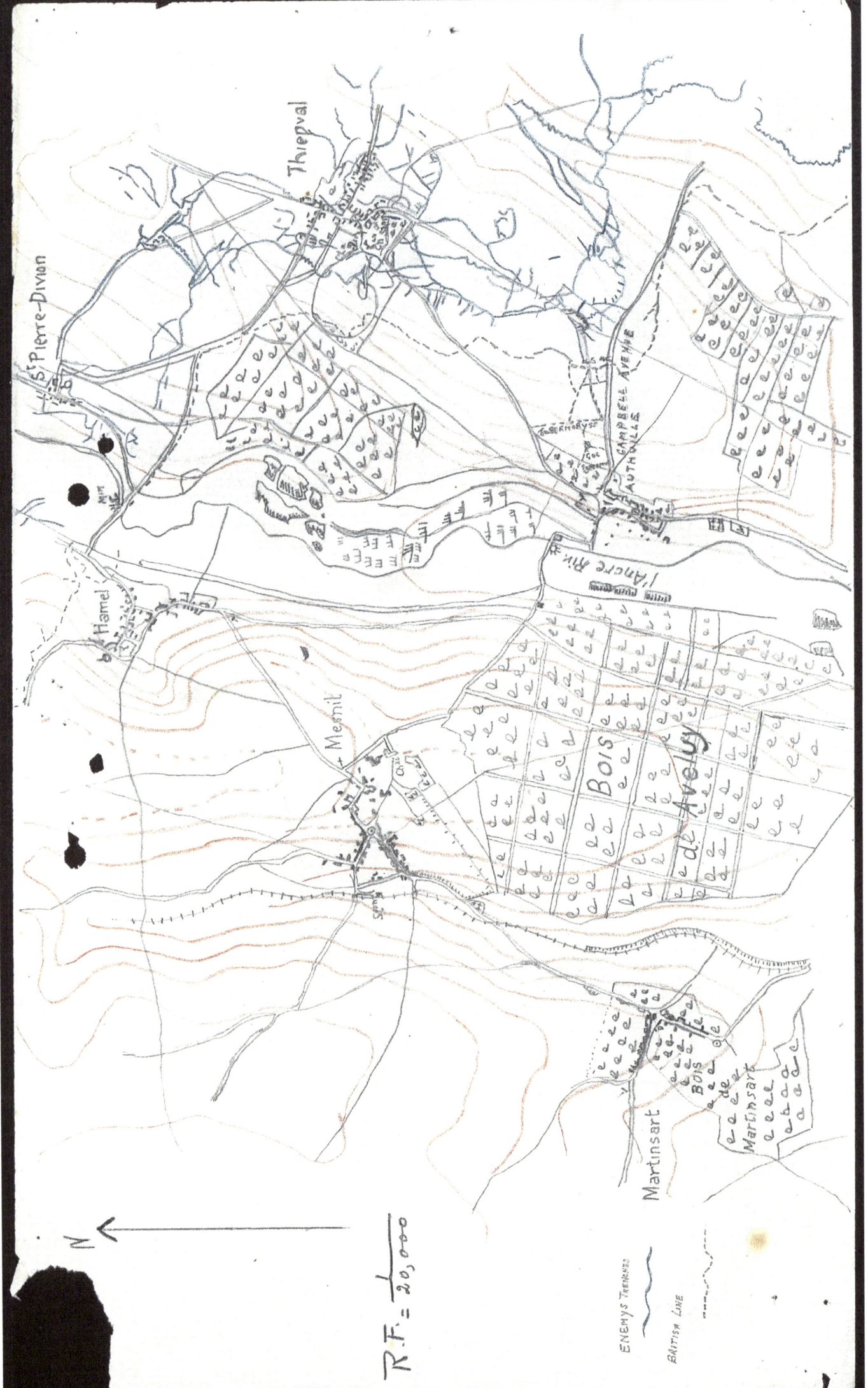

SERIAL No. 71

Confidential

War Diary

of

1st King's Dragoon Guards.

FROM 1st October 1915 TO 31st December 1915

Army Form C. 2118

WAR DIARY
or
INTELLIGENCE SUMMARY

(Erase heading not required.)

Instructions regarding War Diaries and Intelligence Summaries are contained in F.S. Regs., Part II. and the Staff Manual respectively. Title Pages will be prepared in manuscript.

Place	Date	Hour	Summary of Events and Information	Remarks and references to Appendices
AUTHIEUX	2.10.15.		6 N.C.Os. and men and 6 horses arrived from Base. 5 horses transferred to Mobile Veterinary Section.	
"	9.10.15.		24 N.C.Os. and men arrived from Base.	
"	13.10.15.		The regiment and A Echelon paraded at 1.30.p.m. and marched to new billet at BERNAVILLE arriving at 2.15.p.m. Two wagons from C.C., A.S.C. and 1 from Brigade Hdqtrs: were sent to move B Echelon baggage to new billets. Capt: L.W.Alexander arrived from England and posted to D Sqdn:	
BERNAVILLE	14.10.15.		10 men and 10 horses transferred to 29th Lancers as batmen. 4 men and 4 horses transferred to 36th J.Horse as batmen. 16 pack cobs arrived from Base for carrying the pack for the new machine guns.	
"	15.10.15.		Capt: L.W.Alexander evacuated to hospital (accidentally shot)	
"	16.10.15		Lieut: Col: J.A.Bell-Smyth proceeded to 3rd Cavalry Brigade to assume command. Major H.J.Williams assumed command of regiment and appointed Tempy: Lieut: Col: Capt: G.R.H.Cheape assumed duties of senior major	
"	17.10.15.		5 N.C.Os. and men, 9 riding and 2 L.D. horses arrived from Base.	
"	18.10.15.		The B Echelon wagons rejoined at 5.30.p.m. from OCCOCHES.	
"	22.10.15.		The Regiment paraded at 8.0.a.m. and marched to the Brigade rendezvous at CANAPLES. At 10.30.a.m. the Brigade marched via VIGNACOURT- PICQUIGNY to a new billeting area. The regiment reached new billets at 3.30.p.m. and went into billets as follows.	

Army Form C. 2118

WAR DIARY
or
INTELLIGENCE SUMMARY
(Erase heading not required.)

Instructions regarding War Diaries and Intelligence Summaries are contained in F. S. Regs., Part II. and the Staff Manual respectively. Title Pages will be prepared in manuscript.

Place	Date	Hour	Summary of Events and Information	Remarks and references to Appendices
BERNAVILLE	22.10.15.		A & C Sqdns: M.Gun & R.H.Q. in MOLLIENS VIDAME. B Sqdn: DREUIL. D Sqdn: CAMPS. B Echelon, Under Capt: W.T.Wells, paraded at 6.30.a.m. and marching by the same route as the Brigade reached new billets at 4.0.p.m. S.S.M.Arney proceeded to the 28th Division on promotion to 2nd Lieutenant in the 2nd Batt: Royal Lancasters.	
MOLLIENS VIDAME	23.10.15.		Capt: R.C.Longworth arrived from England and posted to A Sqdn:	
"	24.10.15.		B Sqdn: evacuated DREUIL, and took up new billets at CAMPS with D Sqdn:	
"	25.10.15.		Capt: A.A.Crossley proceeded to 3rd Cavalry Brigade as A.D.C. to the G.O.C. 2 men and 4 horses proceeded to the 3rd Cavalry Brigade. 100 N.C.Os. and men (dismounted reinforcements) arrived from Base.	
"	26.10.15.		Lieut: E.W.H.Sprot and 2nd Lieut: R.S.Adair, arrived from Base and posted to B Sqdn:	
"	27.10.15.		16 N.C.Os. and men. 38 riding horses. 2 L.D.horses and 2 chargers arrived from Base. 5 horses transferred to Mobile Veterinary Section.	
"	28.10.15.		2nd Lieut: J.P.Moreton arrived from the Base and posted to C Sqdn:	
"	31.10.15.		8 men. 2 chargers and 1 pack pony arrived from Base.	
"	2.11.15.		2nd Lieut: W.S.H.Parker arrived from Base and posted to D Sqdn:	
"	3.11.15.		3 men and 6 chargers arrived from Base.	
"	6.11.15.		4 men arrived from Base. 3 horses and 2 mules transferred to Mobile Veterinary Section.	

Army Form C. 2118.

WAR DIARY
INTELLIGENCE SUMMARY
(Erase heading not required.)

Instructions regarding War Diaries and Intelligence
Summaries are contained in F. S. Regs., Part II.
and the Staff Manual respectively. Title pages
will be prepared in manuscript.

Hour, Date, Place	Summary of Events and Information	Remarks and references to Appendices
	ration on the man, and two days ration on the troop pack saddle. The forage ration which could be carried, was un-consumed portion of previous day' ration in nose bag and hay net: 12 pounds of corn in the corn sack and 1 pound of goor was issued as an emergency ration. B Echelon remained parked at Bde. H.Q. xxxxx MAMETZ and in the event of a move forward they were to dump all kits there, draw 2 days rations from AIRE, and rejoin Bde. rendezvous; meanwhile the lorries were to feed us direct, as long as roads permitted, A Echelon would then carry on, refilling from the lorries, and fix finally the Brigades would have to live on what they could carry.	The officers who accompanied the regiment to the trenches were Lt. Col Bell-Smyth. A Sqdn Capt Cheape. Lt. Carleton-Smith 2/" Murray-Johnson B " Major Hunt. Lt. Ward. 2/" Farthing. C " Capt. Renton. " Cooper, Lt. Grattan-Holt D " Capt. Alexander Lt. Hatfeild " Wilson. Actg. Adjt. Major Turner.
RINCQ 27.5.15	The Brigade marched at 9.30 a.m. to billets at OXELAERE A and B Echelons accompanying the regiment.	
OXELAERE 28.5.15.	The regiment marched with B. Echelon at 6.30 a.m. to ERKELSBRUGGE where B Echelon and the horses were left in billets. A Echelon marched at 5 a.m. to VLAMERTINGHE. At 1.30 p.m. 275 officers and men, including Maxim Gun detachment, proceeded from ERKELSBRUGGE to billets in huts S.W. of VLAMERTINGHE where A Echelon joined them. Three officers per squadron accompanied the regiment, the remainder stayed in charge of horses. That evening the whole of the first Indian Cavalry Division was concentrated in these huts.	Major Hunt was hit going up in ZOUAVE WOOD and Lt. Ward commanded B. On the evening of the 1st, Col Bell_Smyth took over command of the Left sub-section and Major Turner took over command of the regiment.
VLAMERTINGE 31.5.15	At 5.15 p.m. the regiment received orders to proceed at once to the front line trench held by the 3rd Dragoon Guards near HOOGE and from thence to attack, and hold the Chateau of HOOGE. The C.O., Squadron Leaders, and Adjt. went on ahead to reconnoitre by daylight and the regiment marched at 6.45 p.m. with A Echelon via YPRES to the ZOUAVE WOOD, S.W. of HOOGE. On arrival of the C.O. at HOOGE a	

Army Form C. 2118

WAR DIARY
or
INTELLIGENCE SUMMARY
(Erase heading not required.)

Instructions regarding War Diaries and Intelligence Summaries are contained in F.S. Regs., Part II. and the Staff Manual respectively. Title Pages will be prepared in manuscript.

Place	Date	Hour	Summary of Events and Information	Remarks and references to Appendices
MOLLIENS VIDAME	8.11.15.		4 horses transferred to Mobile Veterinary Section.	
"	9.11.15.		No:1311 Sgt: Davison and 586 Cpl: Waterman decorated by the French authorities with the Croix de Guerre for gallantry at HOOGE.	
"	12.11.15.		2 chargers arrived from Base.	
"	14.11.15.		3 horses transferred to Mobile Veterinary Section.	
"	15.11.15.		Capt: R.C.Longworth and 2nd Lieut: J.P.Moreton proceeded to 5th Division for attachment to Infantry for one month.	
"	18.11.15.		The regiment and A Echelon paraded at 12.30.p.m. and marched via MORTAGNE and LE QUESNOY to LONGPRE, where they went into billets at 2.30.p.m. B Echelon, under lieut: R.G. Fox, and the dismounted men under 2nd Lieut: W.S.H.Parker R.S. Adair marched from a rendezvous at the cross roads half mile South of the 2nd L in LE FAYEL to the new billeting area independently.	
LONGPRE. "	22.11.15.		8 horses and 1 mule arrived from Base.	
"	2.12.15.		No: 5118 R.S.M.Brewer gazetted 2nd: Lieutenant, and posted to C Sqdn.	
"	4.12.15.		3 horses arrived from Base.	
"	6.12.15.		4 men arrived from Base.	
"	16.12.15.		The Regiment marched to a Brigade rendezvous at a point half mile south-west of DUNCQ, whence the Brigade marched at 10.30.a.m. via LIERCOURT - BRAY - LAREUIL to CAMBRON. At CAMBRON the regiments of the Brigade marched independently to new billets.	

Army Form C. 2118.

WAR DIARY
or
INTELLIGENCE SUMMARY.
(Erase heading not required.)

Instructions regarding War Diaries and Intelligence Summaries are contained in F. S. Regs., Part II. and the Staff Manual respectively. Title pages will be prepared in manuscript.

Place	Date	Hour	Summary of Events and Information	Remarks and references to Appendices
LONGPRE	16.12.15.		The regiment arrived at new area at 2.0.p.m. and went into billets as follows:- D Sqdn: CAHON. A,B & C Sqdns: QUESNOY LE MONTANT. M.Gun and Regtl: Hdqtrs: LE MONTANT. A Echelon, under Capt: W.T.Wells marched in rear of the regiment and went into billets as above; B Echelon, under Lieut: R.G.Fox. marched at 7.45.a.m. by the same route as the regiment, arriving at new billets at 5.0.p.m. LONGPRE 20 dismounted men under Lieut: W.H.Parker paraded at the Place. LONGPRE at 11.30.a.m. and proceeded to ABBEVILLE by train, thence marching to new billets arriving at 6.0.p.m.	
LE MONTANT	21.12.15.		3 N.C.Os. and men arrived from Base.	
"	25.12.15.		Major R.S.Hunt arrived from England and assumed the duties of Senior major. (Tempy:) Major Cheape reverted to substantive rank of Captain, and assumed command of A Sqdn; ***************************************	

"	31.12.15.		Strength of regiment on 31.12.15.
			
			Officers. 30. Riding horses 587.
			O.Ranks. 513. Draught " 8.
			    " 79.* Pack " 28.
			
			                                    Mules 64.
			
			*Of new establishment of 100 dismounted reinforcements serving with regiment.	

Army Form C. 2118.

WAR DIARY
or
INTELLIGENCE SUMMARY.

(Erase heading not required.)

Place	Date	Hour	Summary of Events and Information	Remarks and references to Appendices
	31.12.15.		Nominal roll of officers serving with regiment 31.12.15.	

Lieut: Colonel.   H.J. Williams.   2nd Lieut: B. Gratton-Holt.
Major.   H.S. Hunt.   "   J.L. Waggett.
Capt: G.R.H. Cheape.   "   A. Brown.
  "   P.S. Spurrier.   "   W.S.H. Parker.
  "   H.A. Wienholt.   "   A. Jacques.
  "   E.T. Harvey.   "   L. Farthing.
Capt: & Adjt: W.H.F. Cooper.   "   R.S. Adair.
Capt: H.M. Fleming.   "   J.P. Moreton.
                   R.G. Longworth.   "   T.H. Chalmers.
Tempy: H.G. Fox.   "   W. Langford.
Lieut: @ T.H. Gladstone.   "   J.P. Brewer.
  "   H.S. Hatfeild.
  "   B.M. Ward.   Capt: & Qr. Mr. W.T. Wells.
  "   F.W.F. Card.
  "   W.H. Muir.   Capt: T.H. Holroyd. R.A.M.C.
  "   C.E. Wilson.

@ Lieut: E.W.H. Sprot.

A.J.Williams   Lieut: Colonel.

Comdg: 1st: King's Dragoon Guards.

SERIAL NO. 71.

Confidential

War Diary

of

1st King's Dragoon Guards.

FROM 1st January 1916 TO 31st January 1916

Army Form C. 2118.

WAR DIARY
or
INTELLIGENCE SUMMARY

(Erase heading not required.)

Instructions regarding War Diaries and Intelligence Summaries are contained in F. S. Regs., Part II. and the Staff Manual respectively. Title pages will be prepared in manuscript.

Hour, Date, Place		Summary of Events and Information	Remarks and references to Appendices
QUESNOY-LE-MONTANT.	9.1.16.	1 charger, 1 horse and 1 mule to Mobile Veterinary Section.	
"	10.1.16.	5 N.C.O's and men proceeded to G.H.Q. for attachment to the 28th Batt: London Regt: prior to entering the Cadet School, with a view to getting commissions.	
"	11.1.16.	A dismounted trench squadron composed of 1 Major, 1 Captain, 4 Sub-alterns and 300 N.C.O's and men (which had been previously organised with machine guns, etc., as part of a Cavalry dismounted division so as to be ready for trench work in case of emergency) commenced a series of route marches on foot with their kits carried knapsack fashion on their backs.	
"	15.1.16.	S.S.M.Liddell promoted 2nd Lieutenant and posted to the 14th: Batt: Durham Light Infantry. Authy-List No.64. d/8.1.16.	
"	18.1.16.	14 R.Horses and 2 chargers arrived from the Base. Lieut:R.G.Fox proceeded to School of Gunnery, prior to transfer to the Royal Artillery.	
"	25.1.16.	28 N.C.O's and men arrived from the Base.	
"	26.1.16.	37 men passed the 1st two tests at Bombing, and thereby qualified themselves to compete for the final test with live grenades. Previous to this 32 men of the regiment had already passed with live grenades, for which they are permitted to wear a grenade badge on the left arm.	
"	28.1.16.	4 horses to Mobile Veterinary Section.	
"	29.1.16.	The Dismounted trench regiment practiced an attack under the General on trenches which had been previously prepared.	

1:17 W 3299—200,000 (E) 8/14 J.B.C. & A.   Forms/C. 2118/11.

Army Form C. 2118.

WAR DIARY
or
INTELLIGENCE SUMMARY

(Erase heading not required.)

Instructions regarding War Diaries and Intelligence Summaries are contained in F. S. Regs., Part II. and the Staff Manual respectively. Title pages will be prepared in manuscript.

Hour, Date, Place		Summary of Events and Information	Remarks and references to Appendices
QUESNOY-LE-MONTANT.	30.1.16.	4 R.Horses and 1 mule arrived from the Base.	
"	30.1.16.	50 horses proceeded to the Royal Canadian Dragoons to be attached thereto for two weeks.	
"	31.1.16.	The machine guns of the Regiemnt were detached, and formed, with the guns of the other two Regiments in the Brigade, into a Machine Gun Squadron.	
	3.1.16.		

Lieut: Colonel.
Comdg. 1st: King's Dragoon Guards.

Army Form C. 2118.

WAR DIARY
or
INTELLIGENCE SUMMARY.

(Erase heading not required.)

Summary of Events and Information

Supplementary to the Entries for November 1915.

No. 526. Cpl: Waterman awarded the Croix de Guerre for:-
Conspicuous gallantry in leading a counter attack on the stables at HOOGE, on the 2nd June.1915.

No. 1311. Sgt: Davis awarded the Croix de Guerre for:-
Whilst in the annexe at HOOGE after the officer and all the men at the post had been killed or wounded he continued alone an energetic defence and afterwards under a heavy fire helped to bring in some wounded men, on the 2nd June.1915.
....

SERIAL NO. 71

Confidential

War Diary

of

1st King's Dragoon Guards

FROM 1st February 1918 TO 29th February 1918

Army Form C. 2118.

WAR DIARY
or
INTELLIGENCE SUMMARY.

(Erase heading not required.)

Instructions regarding War Diaries and Intelligence Summaries are contained in F. S. Regs., Part II and the Staff Manual respectively. Title pages will be prepared in manuscript.

Place	Date	Hour	Summary of Events and Information	Remarks and references to Appendices
QUESNOY-LE-MONTANT.	3.2.16.		Captain.L.W.Alexander rejoined the regiment. 2/Lieuts:L.G.L.Peacocke,R.I.Ward, and G.G.L.Tiarks arrived.	
"	9.2.16.		13 men passed the Final Test as Grenadiers making the total of 42 Grenadiers in the Regiment.	
"	14.2.16.		11 men passed the Final Test as Grenadiers bringing total to 53.	
"	15.2.16.		4 men, 8 chargers, and 10 Riding horses arrived from the Base.15.2.16.	
"	17.2.16.		Two, digging parties, one of 2 Officers and 57 men, and the other of 1 Officer and 51 men, proceeded to Mulhead.CAMACIES, to be attached to 7th and 17th Corps respectively: Captain Alexander and Lieut:W.H.Muir being in charge of the party for the 7th, and Lieut:F.W.F.Card for the 17th.	
"	18.2.16.		The party for the 17th Corps arrived at their destination on morning of 18th and went into camp in huts about 3 or 4 miles behind the firing line and were employed at first improving the camp. On 20th they commenced work cleaning out old trenches and building dug-outs etc; working daily in 2 reliefs from 8.30.am to 12.30.pm. and from 12.30. to 4.30pm. Some men were also employed in putting up huts in other Camps. The party with the 7th Corps were billeted elsewhere & employed on similar work.	
QUESNOY-LE-MONTANT.	19.2.16.		23 N.C.Os and men arrived from the Base.	
"	22.2.16.		10 N.C.Os and men passed the Final Test as Grenadiers: Total.63.	

Lieut:Colonel:
Comdg: 1st King's Dragoon Guards.
5.3.16.

No: 2164 Pte: Burdett died in hospital CALLAIS.

Supplementary. 10th November 1914.

SERIAL NO. 71

Confidential
War Diary
of

1st King's Dragoon Guards

FROM 1st March 1916 TO 31st March 1916.

Army Form C. 2118.

WAR DIARY
or
INTELLIGENCE SUMMARY.
(Erase heading not required.)

Instructions regarding War Diaries and Intelligence Summaries are contained in F. S. Regs., Part II. and the Staff Manual respectively. Title pages will be prepared in manuscript.

Place	Date	Hour	Summary of Events and Information	Remarks and references to Appendices
QUESNOY LE MONTANT.	2.3.16.		Lieut: W.S.H.Parker rejoined the regiment after being attached to the infantry for one month's duty in the trenches.	
"	10.3.16.	"	Lieut: F.W.F.Card and 51 N.C.Os and men digging party attached to 17th Corps, rejoined the regiment.	
"	22.3.16.	"	22 N.C.Os and men arrived from the Base. Captain: L.W.Alexander, Lieut: W.H.Muir and 57 N.C.Os and men, digging party attached to 7th Corps, rejoined the regiment.	
"	25.3.16.	"	No.4306.L/Cpl: Rea 1st K.D.Gds promoted 2nd Lieut: with effect from 19th March.1916, after attending a course at the Cadet School, and posted to the 7th Batt: Suffolk Regiment. No.3635.Pte: J.McArthur. No.9242.L/Cpl: Jackson. No.3655.Pte: Broom and No.3654.Pte: Harvey 1st K.D.Gds promoted temporary 2nd lieuts: with effect from 19th March.1916 after attending a course at the Cadet School, and posted to 15th Batt: Royal Scots: 7th Batt: East Yorks Regt: and the two last named to 2nd Batt: Seaforth Highlanders.	
"	26.3.16.	"	The Regiment marched at 9.15.a.m. to a Brigade rendezvous at BONNEVAL, thence the Brigade marched via BUIGNY, LE PLESSIEL and CANCHY to a new billeting area at AUXI LE CHATEAU. The Regiment arrived, and went into billets at GUESCHART, at 2.0.p.m. A Echelon under Capt: W.T. Wells marched via THOISON, PT 67, and CANCHY to the new billets arriving shortly after the regiment. B Echelon under Lieut: R.S.Adair marched at 6.45.a.m. to a Brigade rendezvous at CAMBRON, and marching by the same route as A Echelon, arrived in the new billets at 4.30.p.m. 30 dismounted N.C.Os and men under Lieut: F.W.F.Card entrained at LE MONTANT At 8.30.a.m. and proceeded by train to AUXI LE CHATEAU, thence marching to the new billets, arriving at 5.0.p.m.	
"	27.3.16.	"	3 men arrived from the Base.	

Army Form C. 2118.

WAR DIARY
or
INTELLIGENCE SUMMARY.

(Erase heading not required.)

Place	Date	Hour	Summary of Events and Information	Remarks and references to Appendices
GUESCLART.	31.3.16.		1 Troop A Sqdn: 1/1st Northants Yeomanry. 1 Troop C Sqdn: North Irish Horse and 1 Troop B Sqdn: 1/1st Yorkshire Dragoons arrived, for attachment to the regiment for one month, to undergo a refresher course in training, and posted to A, C, and B Sqdns respectively.	

Major.

Comdg: 1st King's Dragoon Guards.

SERIAL NO. 71.

Confidential

War Diary

of

1st King's Dragoon Guards

FROM 1st April 1916 TO 30th April 1916.

Army Form C. 2118.

WAR DIARY
or
INTELLIGENCE SUMMARY.

(Erase heading not required.)

Instructions regarding War Diaries and Intelligence Summaries are contained in F. S. Regs., Part II. and the Staff Manual respectively. Title pages will be prepared in manuscript.

Copy for D.A. 3rd Echelon

Place	Date	Hour	Summary of Events and Information	Remarks and references to Appendices
GUESCHART.	1.4.16.		Lieut: W.Langford. proceeded to Field Company R.E's 55th Division, to instruct in horsemastership.	
"	2.4.16.		13 men arrived from the Base.	
"	8.4.16.		33 horses arrived from the Base.	
"	9.4.16.		The Regiment marched via NOYELLE - GAPENNES to NEUF MOULIN, to a Brigade Training area, and carried out Squadron, Regimental, and Brigade Training daily. A Echelon and a part of B Echelon under Lieut:R.S.Adair accompanied the regiment, whilst a few Details and sick horses remained behind in billets.	
"	12.4.16.		2nd Lieut:A.Jacques appointed Adjutant to the 1st Indian Cavalry Divisional School, and proceeded to VACQUERIETTE to take up his appointment.	
NEUF MOULIN.	13.4.16.		Lieut:R.C.Longworth proceeded to the 1st: Res: Regiment of Cavalry.	
"	15.4.16.		The Regiment returned to permanent billets at GUESCHART.	
GUESCHART.	17.4.16.		14 men arrived from the Base.	
"	17.4.16.		2nd Lieut:T.H.Chalmers appointed instructor in Sniping at 1st Ind: Cav: Divl: School at VACQUERIETTE.	
"	20.4.16.		Sgt: McConnon to Divisional School as acting Q.M.S.	
"	23.4.16.		20 horses arrived from the Base.	
"	24.4.16.		No.3682.Pte: J.Shiels 1st K.D.G'ds promoted temporary 2nd Lieut:(on probation) with effect from 23.4.16, after attending a course at the Cadet School.	

Army Form C. 2118.

WAR DIARY
or
INTELLIGENCE SUMMARY.
(Erase heading not required.)

Instructions regarding War Diaries and Intelligence Summaries are contained in F. S. Regs., Part II. and the Staff Manual respectively. Title pages will be prepared in manuscript.

Place	Date	Hour	Summary of Events and Information	Remarks and references to Appendices
GUESCHART.	24.4.16.		Lieut:H.S.Hatfield and 10 N.C.Os and men proceeded to the 1st Indian Cav: Divisional School of Instruction, to undergo training in courses of Hotchkiss gun, Sniping, Anti-Gas and Bombing.	
"	27.4.16.		2nd Lieut:W.S.Parker proceeded to the Signal Sqdn:1st Ind: Cav: Division to undergo a course of signalling.	
"	28.4.16.		10 N.C.Os and men passed the final test as bombers, bringing the total strength of Bombers in the Regiment to 72.	
"	30.4.16.		Lieut:E.W.H.Sprot.Lieut:F.W.F.Card and 2nd Lieut:G.G.E.Tiarks, and 8 N.C.O and men proceeded to the 1st Indian Cavalry Divisional School of Instruction, to undergo training in courses of Hotchkiss gun, Sniping, Anti-Gas and Bombing. Lieut:H.S.Hatfield and 10 N.C.Os and men returned from the 1st Ind: Cav: Divl:School. Lieut:W.Langford rejoined from Field Company,R.E's, 55th Division. Capt:H.M.Fleming rejoined from Divisional Staff.	

Supplement to "War Diary"

Awards.   MILITARY CROSS.   Sergt: Major: Richard Holmes.
(1st King's Dragoon Guards.)

Major.
Comdg: 1st King's Dragoon Guards.

SERIAL NO. 71

Confidential

War Diary

of

1st King's Dragoon Guards.

FROM 1st July 1916 TO 31st August 1916.

Army Form C. 2118.

WAR DIARY
or
INTELLIGENCE SUMMARY.
(Erase heading not required.)

Instructions regarding War Diaries and Intelligence Summaries are contained in F. S. Regs., Part II. and the Staff Manual respectively. Title pages will be prepared in manuscript.

Place	Date	Hour	Summary of Events and Information	Remarks and references to Appendices
GUESCHART.	1.5.16.		The Regiment marched via YVRENCH, to ST RICQUER to attend a week's Divisional Training. A Echelon and part of B Echelon accompanied the Regiment.	
ST RICQUER.	5.5.16.		Capt: G.R.H. Cheape proceeded to the 1/7th Batt: Royal Highlanders. Capt: H.M. Fleming assumed Command of A Sqdn: vice Capt: Cheape.	
"	7.5.16.		The Regiment returned to permanent billets at GUESCHART. 13 Riding horses and 1 mule arrived from the Base.	
GUESCHART.	10.5.16.		The Regiment marched at 7.45.a.m. via LE DOIGLE - BUIRE AU BOIS - VACQUERIETTE-le-Boucq and FREVENT, to new billets at SERICOURT and SIBIVILLE arriving at 12.15.p.m. A.Echelon under 2.S.M. Browning proceeded by the same route and arrived shortly after the Regiment. B Echelon under 2nd Lieut: R.S.Adair arrived at the new billets at 3.0.p.m.	
SERICOURT.	11.5.16.		2nd Lieut: L.Farthing proceeded to Headqtrs: VII Corps, as an Instructor in Horsemanship.	
"	14.5.16.		Lieut: W.H. Muir proceeded to the 55th Division for the purpose of instructing in Horsemastership.	
"	15.5.16.		2nd Lieut: R.S.Adair proceeded to Ammunition Railhead, to take up permanent duties as Ammunition Supply Officer.	
"	21.5.16.		Lieut: Colonel: H.J.Williams proceeded to England.	
"	24.5.16.		Lieut: Colonel: H.F. Wickham assumed Command of the Regiment. 5 N.C.Os and men arrived from the Base. The Regiment being allowed a compliment of Hotchkiss guns, the first consignment of 6 guns with pack horses being completed, teams are now in training.	

2353 Wt. W3544/1454 700,000 5/15 D.D. & L. A.D.S.S./Forms/C. 2118.

Army Form C. 2118.

WAR DIARY
or
INTELLIGENCE SUMMARY.

(Erase heading not required.)

Instructions regarding War Diaries and Intelligence Summaries are contained in F.S. Regs., Part II. and the Staff Manual respectively. Title pages will be prepared in manuscript.

Place	Date	Hour	Summary of Events and Information	Remarks and references to Appendices
SERICOURT.	24.5.16.		The Regiment received orders to remain in a state of readiness to move within four hours of notification.	
"	25.5.16.		The Regiment paraded for an inspection by the Commander-in-Chief.	
"	29.5.16.		2nd Lieut: A.Brown, 7 N.C.Os and men proceeded to the 1st Indian Cavalry Divisional School of Instruction to undergo courses of training in Bombing, Hotchkiss gun, Anti-Gas, and Sniping.	
"	30.5.16.		12 N.C.Os and men arrived from the Base.	
			**********************************	
			Supplement to the "War Diary".	

			Brigadier General: Fasken on relinquishing the Command of the Lucknow Cavalry Brigade requested the O.C.K.D.Gds to convey to all ranks of the Regiment his farewell thanks and his best wishes for their future.	

			The Commander-in-Chief, as the result of his inspection wishes to convey to all ranks his satisfaction at the turn out of the 1st Indian Cavalry Division. He considers the horses reflect credit on all concerned and the turn out of the men and saddlery was smart and soldierly.	

WMCorpurept[?] Lieut: Colonel;
Comdg: 1st King's Dragoon Guards.

SERIAL NO. 71

Confidential

War Diary

of

1st King's Liverpool Regiment.

FROM 1st June 1916 TO 30th June 1916

To.
   D.A.G. Ind:Sect:
   3rd Echelon.
   G.H.Q.

                                      Field. 4.7.16.

       Will you please make the following alteration in the "War Diary" for the month of May, 1916, of the Regiment under my Command.

   SERICOURT.   24.5.16.   "Lieut:Colonel:H.F.Wickham assumed Command of the Regiment".

should read:-

   SERICOURT.   24.5.16.   "Lieut:Colonel:H.F.Wickham rejoined and assumed Command of the Regiment from temporary Command of 10th Hussars."

                                      Lieut:Colonel:
                               Comdg: 1st King's Dragoon Guards.

Army Form C. 2118.

WAR DIARY
or
INTELLIGENCE SUMMARY.
(Erase heading not required.)

Instructions regarding War Diaries and Intelligence Summaries are contained in F. S. Regs., Part II. and the Staff Manual respectively. Title pages will be prepared in manuscript.

Place	Date	Hour	Summary of Events and Information	Remarks and references to Appendices
SERICOURT.	1.6.16.		The Regiment has now a complement of 8 Hotchkiss Guns.	
"	2.6.16.		Lieut:C.E.Wilson,2nd Lieuts:Moreton and Waggett, and 7 N.C.Os and men proceeded to the 1st Indian Cavalry Divisional School of Instruction, to undergo courses of Instruction in Bombing, Hotchkiss Gun, Sniping, and Anti-Gas.	
"	4.6.16.		Lieut:H.W.H.Sprot proceeded to the 138th Brigade, 47th Division, to be attached to the infantry for one month's training. Lieut:A.Brown, 7 N.C.Os and men rejoined from Divisional School of Instruction.	
"	5.6.15.		Major:R.S.Hunt proceeded to the 1/4th Batt: Seaforth Highlanders as second in Command. Lieut:L.Tartaining rejoined from duties with the 55th Division.	
"	9.6.16.		Lieut:A.B.Richardson and Lieut:R.G.Fox proceeded to the 1st Indian Cavalry Divisional School of Instruction to undergo a course of Anti-Gas.	
"	9.6.16.		Lieut:F.K.Murray Johnson and 3 N.C.Os proceeded to the 3rd Army School to undergo a course of Bayonet Fighting.	
"	11.6.16.		Lieut:C.E.Wilson, 2nd Lieuts:J.P.Moreton and J.L.Waggett, 7 N.C.Os and men rejoined from 1st Divisional School of Instruction. Lieut:W.Langford rejoined from duties with 55th Division. Capt:& Qr:Mr:W.T.Wells evacuated to hospital.	
"	13.6.16.		2nd Lieut:J.P.Brewer, 50 N.C.Os and men embussed at SERICOURT and proceeded to MARGEUIL, being attached to the 17th Corps. Their work was chiefly general fatigues, unloading trains etc., from 8.0.am to 12 noon and 1.30.pm to 5.0.p.m. For two days they were shelled whilst carrying out their work, but luckily there were no casualties.	
"	15.6.16.		7 R.Horses, 2 pack horses and 1 charger arrived from the Base.	

Army Form C. 2118.

WAR DIARY
or
INTELLIGENCE SUMMARY.

(Erase heading not required.)

Instructions regarding War Diaries and Intelligence Summaries are contained in F. S. Regs., Part II. and the Staff Manual respectively. Title pages will be prepared in manuscript.

Place	Date	Hour	Summary of Events and Information	Remarks and references to Appendices
SERI COURT.	15.6.16.		Capt:R.S.Spurrier, Lieut:R.G.Fox,Lieut:H.S.Hatfield, 2nd Lieut:L.G.L.Peacocke, 200 N.C.Os and men emlussed and proceeded to SQUASTRE, being attached to the 7th Corps. Their work was the burying of telephone wires from Battery positions to the first line trenches, working in small parties from 9.a.m. to 4.0.p.m.each day. For one day they were shelled almost continuously and had to cease work and take cover, but returned without any casualties. The following message received from the 56th Division as regards their work is :- "The C.R.A.56th Division wishes to state that the assistance recently given to the 56th Divisional Artillery by the Cavalry was very much appreciated. Both officers and men worked extremely hard and their services proved invaluable."	
"	16.6.16.		Lieut:F.K.Murray Johnson and 3 N.C.Os rejoined from 3rd Army School.	
"	19.6.16.		Lieut:A.B.Richardson, 2nd Lieut:A.Jacques, 2nd Lieut:T.N.Chalmers and 10 N.C.Os and men rejoined from Divisional School of Instruction.	
"	21.6.16.		2nd Lieut:J.G.K.Barraclough arrived from England and posted to A Sqdn:	
"	24.6.16.		Capt:R.S.Spurrier,Lieut:R.G.Fox, Lieut:H.S.Hatfield, 2nd Lieut:L.G.L.Peacocke and 200 N.C.Os and men rejoined from attachment to 7th Corps. Lieut:W.H.Muir rejoined from duties with 55th Division.	
"	25.6.16.		5 Men arrived from the Base. Lieut:F.W.F.Card evacuated to hospital.	
"	27.6.16.		2nd Lieut:J.P.Brewer,50 N.C.Os and men rejoined from attachment to 17th Corps.	
"	30.6.16.		The Regiment, with A and B Echelons marched at 9.30.a.m. via ARBRE and BOUQUEMAISON to the new billeting area at GROUCHES, arriving at 11.30.a.m. The Dismounted Men under Lieut:R.G.Fox marched at 1.15.p.m. to REBREUVE, and billeted there.	

2353 Wt. W2544/1454 700,000 5/15 D.D.& L. A.D.S.S./Forms/C. 2118.

Army Form C. 2118.

WAR DIARY
or
INTELLIGENCE SUMMARY.

(Erase heading not required.)

Summary of Events and Information

Supplementary to "War Diary".

Extracts from LONDON (AZETTE dated 15th June. 1916.

Colonel: F.C.L.Hulton   R.of O.   "Mentioned in Despatches."
Major: R.M.F.Langton   do   do   do
2nd Lieut: L.Farthing 1.D.Gds.   do   do   do

****

W.M.Cooper   Capt: & Adjt:
                       for
                    Lieut:Colonel:
            Comdg: 1st King's Dragoon Guards.

SERIAL NO. 171

Confidential
War Diary
of
1st King's Dragoon Guards

FROM 1st July 1916 TO 31st July 1916

Army Form C.2118.

WAR DIARY
or
INTELLIGENCE SUMMARY.

(Erase heading not required.)

Instructions regarding War Diaries and Intelligence Summaries are contained in F. S. Regs., Part II. and the Staff Manual respectively. Title pages will be prepared in manuscript.

Place	Date	Hour	Summary of Events and Information	Remarks and references to Appendices
CROUCHES.	1.7.16.		The Regiment received orders to remain in a state of readiness to move within two hours of notification.	
			The Regiment marched at 5.30.p.m. via HAUTE-VISEE - RAMBART - BAILLY into new billets at FROHEN LE GRAND, arriving at 7.45.p.m.	
			A Echelon under S.S.M.Browning arrived shortly after the Regiment.	
			B Echelon under 2nd Lieut:J.G.K.Barraclough marched via HAUTE VISEE - HAUTE, arriving at new billets at 11.30.p.m.	
			Cpl:Rogers 1st K.D.Gds. promoted 2nd Lieut: with effect from 12.6.16.and posted to 15th Batt:Royal Warwick Regiment, after attending a course at the Cadet School.	
FROHEN LE GRAND.	2.7.16.		2nd Lieut:.A.Jacques proceeded to 3rd Army School to take up duties as Adjutant.	
"	5.7.16.		2 Men, 4 chargers,7 riding horses, 4 pack and 1 L.D. arrived from the Base.	
"	7.7.16.		38 N.C.Os and Men passed the Regimental Tests as Hotchkiss Gunners,and granted a badge for same.	
"	9.7.16.		16 N.C.Os and Men, and 10 horses arrived from the Base.	
"	11.7.16.		9 N.C.Os and Men passed the Regt:Tests as H'kiss Gunners and granted the badge.	
			Lieut:R.G.Fox proceeded to England.	
"	14.7.16.		Lieut:F.W.F.Card rejoined from hospital.	
			5 N.C.Os and Men, 20 Riding horses and 3 chargers arrived from the Base.	
"	19.7.16.		The Regiment marched at 8.40.a.m. via BONNIERES-REBREUVIETTE-AUBRINES-SAVY to new billets at CAMBLIGNEUL, arriving at 4.30.p.m.	
			A Echelon under R.Q.M.S.Mackey accompanied the Regiment.	

2353 Wt. W2544/1454 700,000 5/15 D. D. & L. A.D.S.S./Forms/C. 2118.

Army Form C. 2118.

WAR DIARY
or
INTELLIGENCE SUMMARY.
(Erase heading not required.)

Instructions regarding War Diaries and Intelligence Summaries are contained in F. S. Regs., Part II and the Staff Manual respectively. Title pages will be prepared in manuscript.

Place	Date	Hour	Summary of Events and Information	Remarks and references to Appendices
FROHEN LE GRAND.	19.7.16.		B Echelon under 2nd Lieut:J.G.K.Barraclough marched at 7.40.a.m. the same route as the Regiment, and arrived at new billets at 8.30.p.m. The Dismounted Men under Lieut:F.W.F.Card marched at 8.30.a.m. to AUXI LE CHATEAU. Entrained AUXI. Detrained TINCQUES and marched to new billets arriving at 6.30.p.m.	
CAMBLIGNEUL.	20.7.16.		Eight Officers (names as per margin), 300 N.C.Os and Men went into support trenches at NEUVILLE ST VAAST, where they were employed in mining operations in the front line, working in reliefs of 8 hours each.	Capt:E.A.Wienholt. " L.W.Alexander. Lieut:E.W.H.Sprot. " F.W.F.Card. 2nd Lieut:A.Brown. " L.G.L.Peacocke. " R.I.Ward.
"	21.7.16.		9 Men and 2 chargers arrived from the Base.	
NEUVILLE ST VAAST.	22.7.16.		Pte:Fraser of the Trench Party slightly wounded in the face with shrapnel.	
"	24.7.16.		Capt:H.K.Fleming releived Capt:L.W.Alexander, and Lieut:A.B.Richardson releived Lieut:C.E.Wilson at NEUVILLE ST VAAST.	
"	25.7.16.		Lieut:J.G.E.Tiarks releived Lieut:A.Brown.	
"	26.7.16.		Lieut:W.H.Muir releived Lieut:R.I.Ward. Lieut:J.L.Waggett, One N.C.O and four Men attached to 180th Brigade in the front line for sniping duties. Lieut:T.H.Gladstone attached to 180 th Brigade in the trenches at AUX RIETZ for duty on the telephone lines etc.	
"	27.7.16.		Sergt:Thurlow of the Trench Party to hospital (bullet wound in leg.)	
"	28.7.16.		Pte:Smith of the Trench Party to hospital. (shrapnel wound in forehead.)	
CAMBLIGNEUL.	30.7.16.		The Trench Party of Eight Officers, 300 N.C.Os and Men rejoined the Regiment Lieut:T.H.Gladstone, Lieut:J.L.Waggett and 5 O.Ranks rejoined the regiment from the 180th Brigade.	

Army Form C.2118.

WAR DIARY
or
INTELLIGENCE SUMMARY.
(Erase heading not required.)

Instructions regarding War Diaries and Intelligence Summaries are contained in F. S. Regs., Part II. and the Staff Manual respectively. Title pages will be prepared in manuscript.

Place	Date	Hour	Summary of Events and Information	Remarks and references to Appendices
CAMBLIGNEUL.	31.7.16.		The Billeting Party paraded at 2.30.p.m. and proceeded to MONCHY-BRETON.	

M.F. Gosselin Capt.
for Lieut:Colonel:
Comdg: 1st King's Dragoon Guards.

2353 Wt. W2544/1454 700,000 5/15 L, D, & L. A.D.S.S./Forms/C. 2118.

SERIAL NO. 71

Confidential
War Diary
of

1st King's Dragoon Guards

FROM 1st August 1916 TO 31st August 1916.

Army Form C. 2118.

WAR DIARY
or
INTELLIGENCE SUMMARY
(Erase heading not required.)

Instructions regarding War Diaries and Intelligence Summaries are contained in F. S. Regs., Part II. and the Staff Manual respectively. Title Pages will be prepared in manuscript.

Place	Date	Hour	Summary of Events and Information	Remarks and references to Appendices
CAMBLIGNEUL.	1.8.16.		The Regiment marched at 8.15.a.m. via VILLERS CHATEL–MINGOVAL–BETHONSART–FREVILLERS–MAGNICOURT–HOUCOURT to MONCHY BRETON, arriving there at 12 noon. A and B Echelons accompanied the Regiment. 20 N.C.Os and Men proceeded to ANZIN for the purpose of working under the R.Es. who were building Gun Emplacements. Working from 8.30.a.m. till 12.30.p.m. and 1 p.m. till 5.0.p.m. the keenness of the men with their work is shown by the following letter:- to O.C.-K.D.Gds. "I should like to bring to your notice, the very good work done by the 20 men who were attached to a detachment of My squadron at ANZIN. The actual work was dull & uninteresting viz - carrying of materials along trenches. Your men did the work cheerfully and rapidly; I only wish we could say the same of all the parties we have had from time to time, though in the case of your Regiment the work has always been excellent. From. M.Evans.O.C.1st Indian Field Squadron.R.E.	
MONCHY BRETON.	6.8.16.		3 N.C.Os and Men arrived from the Base.	
"	8.8.16.		An Escort Party, consisting of Major:R.S.Spurrier (in command) Capt:Alexander, 2nd Lieut:J.E.Moreton,J.Q.F.Clarke,J.P.Brewer, C Sqdn; 1 troop of A Sqdn; and 1 Section of Machine Guns, marched at 7.0.a.m. 8th ult, to WAVRANS. They were inspected by the King on the morning of the 10th at 9.0.a.m. Three troops in marching order and the Transport in drill order. 20 N.C.Os and Men rejoined from attachment to Field Sqdn: R.Es.	escort & M.G. Troop
"	9.8.16.		The Regiment marched at 7.0.a.m. via BAILLEUL–AVERDOINGT–MAZINGHEM–SARS LES BOIS–BERLENCOURT–WARLUZEL to HURBERCOURT, arriving at 12 noon. A Echelon accompanied the Regiment. B Echelon under 2nd Lieut:J.G.K.Barraclough marched at 6.15.a.m. the same route as the Regiment, and arrived at the new billets at 1.30.p.m. Major:R.S.Spurrier,Capt:L.W.Alexander,2nd Lieuts:J.E.Moreton and J.P.Brewer with C Sqdn: of the Escort Party, rejoined the Regiment.	

Army Form C. 2118.

WAR DIARY
or
INTELLIGENCE SUMMARY
(Erase heading not required.)

Instructions regarding War Diaries and Intelligence Summaries are contained in F. S. Regs., Part II. and the Staff Manual respectively. Title Pages will be prepared in manuscript.

Place	Date	Hour	Summary of Events and Information	Remarks and references to Appendices
HUMBERCOURT.	10.8.16.		Capt:S.E.Harvey (in command),Capt:T.H.Holroyd (R.A.M.C.) Lieut:H.S.Hatfeild 2nd Lieuts:Murray Johnson, L.Farthing,J.P.Moreton,J.G.K.Barraclough, 256 N.C.Os and Men proceeded to POMMIER, being attached to the 138th Infantry Brigade. The work of the party was chiefly the transferring of Gas Cylinders into the front line trenches. 2nd Lieuts:W.Langford,J.G.B.Tiarke,1 Troop of A Sqdn: and 1 Section of Machine Guns rejoined the Regiment from Escort Duty. 9355.Pte:Guthrie wounded in the back, and to hospital.	
"	12.8.16.		A further working party consisting of 2nd Lieut:J.P.Brewer, 38 N.C.Os and Men proceeded to POMMIER.	
"	13.8.16.		Another party of 18 N.C.Os and Men proceeded to POMMIER. 4763.S.Q.M.S.Buxton and 7757.L/Cpl:Drake having obtained their commissions are posted to 5th Batt: Bedfordshire Regiment and 11th Royal Warwick Regt: respectively; after attending a course at the Cadet School.	
"	14.8.16.		The working party of Capt:S.E.Harvey (in command),Capt:T.H.Holroyd,Lieut: H.S.Hatfeild, 2nd Lieuts:F.K.Murray Johnson,L.Farthing,J.P.Brewer,J.P.Moreton,J.G.K.Barraclough,314 N.C.Os and Men rejoined the Regiment. The excellent work done by the party is shown by the following letter from the G.O.C. 46th Division:- "The Major General Commanding 46th Division has instructed me to write to you to inform you of his satisfaction with the good work and cheerfulness in carrying-ing out the work shown by your Regiment, when employed in helping us in carrying operations."J.Thorpe, Lt:Col: 46th Div:.	
"	15.8.16.		S.S.M.Percival proceeded to 33rd Bde:Headqtrs: having obtained his commission, and posted to 6th Border Regiment. 2nd Lieut:R.McColough joined from the 1st Res:Regt: of Cavalry. 9 N.C.Os and Men arrived from the Base.	

Army Form C. 2118.

WAR DIARY
or
INTELLIGENCE SUMMARY
(Erase heading not required.)

Instructions regarding War Diaries and Intelligence Summaries are contained in F. S. Regs., Part II. and the Staff Manual respectively. Title Pages will be prepared in manuscript.

Place	Date	Hour	Summary of Events and Information	Remarks and references to Appendices
HUMBERCOURT.	16.8.16.		A Sniping party consisting of Lieut:W.H.Muir, 2nd Lieut:J.L.Waggett, 13 N.C.Os and Men proceeded to BAILLEULMONT for attachment with the 137th Brigade for duty in the front line trenches.	
"	18.8.16.		Capt:L.W.Alexander, 14 N.C.Os and Men with 4 Hotchkiss Guns, proceeded to BAILLACOURT for duty with the 139th Brigade in the trenches. The keenness of the party was shown by the following letter:- "I should like to bring to the notice of the Brigadier General the fact that the N.C.Os and Men of the King's Dragoon Guards Hotchkiss Gun Detachment under Capt:L.W.Alexander who were attached to my Battalion in the trenches from the 18th to 22nd inst, displayed great keenness in their work. On two occasions at night I sent a Hotchkiss Gun with a strong patrol into No Man's Land, and although these patrols had not the luck to come across enemy patrols the officer i/c commented on the coolness and reliability of the gun teams. Sd/- G.D.Goodman.Lt:Col: Comdg: 6th Sherwood Foresters. Lieut:H.S.Hatfield, 14 N.C.Os and Men with 4 Hotchkiss Guns proceeded to BRETONCOURT, being attached to the 139th Brigade for duty in the trenches. 9 Men and 8 horses arrived from the Base.	
"	22.8.16.		Cpl:White of the Snipers party wounded in the leg and to hospital. Major:R.S.Spurrier (in command) Lieut:F.W.F.Card, 2nd Lieuts:A.Brown,R.I.Ward, R.McCollough, 162 N.C.Os and Men proceeded to SAILLY AU BOIS for work with the 181st Tunnelling Company. The party worked in 6 hour reliefs, half from 8.45.p.m. till 2.45.a.m. and the other half from 2.45.a.m. till 8.45a.m.They were employed in mining operations beyond HABUTERNE. A daily working party composed of 2nd Lieut:W.Langford, 129 N.C.Os and Men proceeding to LUCHEUX WOOD every morning, were employed in making hurdles etc, for the revetting of trenches, under instructions from the R.Es.	
"	23.8.16.		Lieut:W.H.Muir, 2nd Lieut:J.L.Waggett, 12 N.C.Os and Men of the sniping party rejoined from 137th Brigade. Capt:L.W.Alexander, 14 N.C.Os and Men of the Hotchkiss Party rejoined from 139th Brigade.	

Army Form C. 2118.

WAR DIARY
or
INTELLIGENCE SUMMARY

(Erase heading not required.)

Instructions regarding War Diaries and Intelligence Summaries are contained in F. S. Regs., Part II. and the Staff Manual respectively. Title Pages will be prepared in manuscript.

Place	Date	Hour	Summary of Events and Information	Remarks and references to Appendices
HUMBERCOURT.	26.8.16.		2nd Lieut:J.P.Brewer relieved 2nd Lieut:W.Langford in command of the daily working party. at LUCHEUX WOOD. 1 N.C.O.,2 Men,5 horses and 1 Mule arrived from the Base. Pte:Clifford wounded in the foot and to hospital.	
"	27.8.16.		2nd Lieut:W.Langford relieved 2nd Lieut:A.Brown with the working party attached to 181st Tunnelling Company at SAILLY AU BOIS.	
"	28.8.16.		2nd Lieut:A.Brown proceeded to CAULLY to attend a course of instruction at the 46th Division Bombing School. Lieut:H.S.Hatfeild 14 N.C.Os and Men with 4 Hotchkiss Guns rejoined from 139th Brigade.	
"	29.8.16.		Capt:E.A.Wienholt relieved Major.R.S.Spurrier in command of the working party at SAILLY AU BOIS.	
"	30.8.16.		2nd Lieut:L.Farming relieved 2nd Lieut:R.I.Ward at SAILLY AU BOIS. 2nd Lieut:J.G.E.Tinne's relieved Lieut:J.W.F.Card at the same place. the regiment has now been completed with 16 hotchkiss guns	
	31.8.16		3 men rejoined from attachment to the machine gun typschre	

Lieut:Colonel:
Comdg: 1st King's Dragoon Guards.

SERIAL NO. 1/1.

Confidential

War Diary

of

1st King's Dragoon Guards.

FROM 1st September, 1916 TO 30th September, 1916.

Army Form C. 2118.

WAR DIARY
or
INTELLIGENCE SUMMARY
(Erase heading not required.)

Instructions regarding War Diaries and Intelligence Summaries are contained in F.S. Regs., Part II. and the Staff Manual respectively. Title Pages will be prepared in manuscript.

Place	Date	Hour	Summary of Events and Information	Remarks and references to Appendices
HUMBERCOURT.	2.9.16.		5 Men, 4 chargers, 12 horses, and 2 mules arrived from the Base. Capt:E.A.Wienholt,2nd Lieuts:L.Farthing,W.Langford,J.G.E.Tiarks,R.L.Mc-Collough,159 N.C.Os and Men rejoined from SAILLY MU BOIS, where they had been employed on tunnelling work in the front line trenches opposite HEBUTURNE.	
"	3.9.16.		The Regiment marched at 8.30.a.m. via LUCHEUX-BOUQUE MAISON-NEUVILLETTE to new billets at MEZEROLLES, arriving there at 12 noon. B Echelon marched at 8.30.a.m., by the same route and arrived one hour after the Regiment. The Dismounted men under Lieut:F.W.F.Card, marched at 6.0.a.m., and arrived at new billets at 12.30.p.m.	
MEZEROLLES.	4.9.16.		The Regiment marched at 8.30.a.m. via FROHEN LE GRAND-BEALCOURT-MAIZICOURT-HEILMONT-YVRENCH to new billets at CANCHY, arriving there at 2.0.p.m. B Echelon under Lieut:J.H.K.Barraclough marched brigaded under the B.T.O. and arrived at new billets at 6.30.p.m. The Dismounted men under Lieut:F.W.F.Card, marched at 8.30.p.m. to BUIRE AU BOIS, where they were billeted, whilst the regiment were training, and from there they were sent to bivouac near MAMETZ (on the Somme front), being employed in making tracks towards the German lines.	
CANCHY.	5.9.16.		Brigade and Divisional Training.	
"	6.9.16.		Brigade and Divisional Training. 12 Pack horses arrived from the Base.	
"	7.9.16.		Brigade and Divisional Training.	
"	8.9.16.		3 chargers, 9 horses and 1 mule arrived from the Base.	
"	9.9.16.		The following letter was received by G.O.C.Lucknow Cav:Brigade from G.O.C. VII Corps.:- The G.O.C. VII Corps has expressed his regret at the departure of the Lucknow Cavalry Brigade from the VII Corps, and his appre-	

2449 Wt. W14957/Mgo 750,000 1/16 J.B.C. & A. Forms/C.2118/12.

Army Form C. 2118.

WAR DIARY
or
INTELLIGENCE SUMMARY
(Erase heading not required.)

Instructions regarding War Diaries and Intelligence Summaries are contained in F.S. Regs., Part II. and the Staff Manual respectively. Title Pages will be prepared in manuscript.

Place	Date	Hour	Summary of Events and Information	Remarks and references to Appendices
CANCHY.	11.9.16.		ciation for the willing services rendered by the Brigade, during its attachment to the Corps. He has thanked Brid:Gen:M.F.GAGE.D.S.O. for the useful reconnaissances of the Army and Corps Lines, carried out by Officers of the Brigade. The Regiment marched at 9.45.a.m. via DOMVAST-BRAILLY-NOYELLE en CHAUSSEE-NEUILLY le DIEN-ACQUET-AUXI. by the main AUXI-DOULLENS road, to FROHEN LE GRAND, a distance of 17 miles, arriving at 12.30.p.m. B Echelon marched brigaded under Lieut:J.H.K.Barraclough, at 8.30.a.m., via GAPENNES-YVRENCH-HEIRMONT-AUXI, arriving at 4.0.p.m.	
FROHEN LE GRAND.	12.9.16.		The Regiment marched at 8.0.a.m. via HEM-HAUTE VISEE to GROUCHES (8 miles) arriving at 10.30.a.m. B Echelon accompanied the Regiment.	
GROUCHES.	13.9.16.		The Regiment paraded at 1.15.p.m. and marched with the Division, via TALMAS-VILLERS BOCAGE-MOLLIENS au BOIS-ST GRATIEN to new camp at QUERRIEUX, arriving there at 7.0.p.m. B Echelon divisionalised marched at 12 noon, and proceeding by the same route as the Regiment, arrived at 11.0.p.m.	
QUERRIEUX.	14.9.16.		Remained in Camp.	
"	15.9.16.		The Regiment paraded at 4.45.a.m., and marched to a preparatory position, bivouacking between MORLANCOURT and BERNANCOURT. B Echelon remained at QUERRIEUX Camp.	
MORLANCOURT CAMP.	16.9.16.		14 N.C.Os and Men arrived from the Base. Ptes:Aitken and Rogers of the dismounted party, wounded in action and to hospital.	
"	18.9.16.		8 N.C.Os arrived from the Base.	
"	19.9.16.		14 horses and 1 pack horse arrived from the Base.	

Army Form C. 2118.

WAR DIARY
or
INTELLIGENCE SUMMARY
(Erase heading not required.)

Instructions regarding War Diaries and Intelligence Summaries are contained in F. S. Regs., Part II and the Staff Manual respectively. Title Pages will be prepared in manuscript.

Place	Date	Hour	Summary of Events and Information	Remarks and references to Appendices
MORLANCOURT CAMP.	20.9.16.		D Sqdn: paraded at 5.0.a.m., and marched to FRICOURT WOOD, where it remained on duty for the day, under orders of the 21st Division, returning to camp at 8.0.p.m.	
"	21.9.16.		Officers patrols were sent out daily to reconnoitre the Cavalry tracks made by our dismounted men towards FLERS,DELVILLE WOOD and LEUZE WOOD.	
"	22.9.16.			
"	23.9.16.			
"	24.9.16.			
"	24.9.16.		Sergt:Alford having obtained his commission proceeded to the 8th Batt: Loyal North Lancs:Regt:	
"	25.9.16.		The Regiment was ordered to "stand to " and be ready to move within ¾ hour's notification. F.Q.M.S.Wooley gazetted to be 2nd Lieut: with effect from 1.9.16. and posted to the Royal Field Artillery.	
"	26.9.16.		The Regiment received orders at 1.0.p.m. to proceed to MAMETZ, where they arrived at 2.20.p.m. At 4.15.p.m. they were ordered to go on to TRONES WOOD, arriving at 5.0.p.m. Established Regimental Report Centre at WATERLOT FARM, about 4000 yards behind the firing line where heavy fighting was in progress. Lieuts:L.Farthing and J.P.Brewer were sent on officers patrols to GUEDECOURT, to gain touch with the Squadron of the 19th Lancers and to report on the situation. No.9881.Pte:Dinsdale B Sqdn: whilst on patrol was wounded, and his horse killed under him. The Regiment withdrew to bivouac at 6.30.p.m. to MONTAUBAN. A Echelon under Major.R.S.Spurrier moved up to MAMETZ.	
MAMETZ.	27.9.16.		The Regiment returned to MAMETZ at 8.0.a.m. and rejoined the remainder of the Brigade. The Regiment marched at 9.0.a.m. to bivouac at BUSSY les DAOURS having halted,halfway for 2½ hours at its old bivouac near MORLANCOURT. Arrived at BUSSY les DAOURS at 6.0.p.m. B Echelon rejoined the Regiment.	

Army Form C. 2118.

WAR DIARY
or
INTELLIGENCE SUMMARY

(Erase heading not required.)

Instructions regarding War Diaries and Intelligence Summaries are contained in F.S. Regs., Part II. and the Staff Manual respectively. Title Pages will be prepared in manuscript.

Place	Date	Hour	Summary of Events and Information	Remarks and references to Appendices
BUSSY les DAOURS.	28.9.16.		The Regiment paraded at 8.0.a.m., and marched via AMIENS-PICQUIGNY to camp at HANGEST.	
HANGEST.	29.9.16.		The Regiment marched at 8.30.a.m. via CONDE-L'ETOILE-COCQUEREL to billets at VAUCHELLES, arriving at 12 noon.	
VAUCHELLES.	30.9.16.		The Regiment marched at 7.15.a.m. via ABBEVILLE to new billets at MACHY, arriving at 11.30.a.m. A Echelon under Lieut: H.S. Hatfeild followed by same route and arrived at 2.0.p.m. B Echelon under Lieut: J.H.K. Barraclough marched at 5.40.a.m. arriving at MACHY at 3.30.p.m.	

W.W. Cooper
Capt: & Adjt:
for
Lieut: Colonel:
Comdg: 1st King's Dragoon Guards.

SERIAL NO. 71.

Confidential
War Diary
of

1st King's Dragoon Guards

FROM 1st October 1916 TO 30th September 3rd October 1915

Army Form C. 2118.

WAR DIARY
or
INTELLIGENCE SUMMARY
(Erase heading not required.)

Instructions regarding War Diaries and Intelligence Summaries are contained in F. S. Regs., Part II and the Staff Manual respectively. Title Pages will be prepared in manuscript.

Place	Date	Hour	Summary of Events and Information	Remarks and references to Appendices
MACHY	1.10.16.		Lieut F.W.F.Card, 2nd Lieut R.I.Ward and 34 dismounted men rejoined from Albert, having been employed in preparing cavalry tracks, and clearing battlefields.	
"	2.10.16.		4. O'Ranks arrived from Base.	
"	5.10.16.		Capt T.H.Holroyd R.A.M.C., attached K.D.Gds: appointed Staff Surgeon to Brigade.	
"	7.10.16.		Lieut: A.B.Richardson evacuated to Hospital. 9 R.Horses and 1. P. Mule arrived from Base.	
"	12.10.16.		2nd Lieut: L. Farthing having been gazetted Lieut: in 2nd Btns: East Lancs: Regt: (to rank for seniority as from 3rd March 1916) proceeded to join that Battalion.	
"	13.10.16.		2nd Lieut: F.K.Murry Johnson proceeded to Bde: Signal Troop to undergo a three months course of signalling.	
"	16.10.16.		5. Men arrived from Base.	
"	20.10.16.		2nd Lieut W.J.P.Dicks arrived from Base and posted to A.Sqdn: A billeting party consisting of Capt: T.H.Holroyd, Lieut T.H.Gladstone Lieut: C.E.Wilson, 2nd Lieut: J.P.Brewer and 25 N.C.Os and men proceeded to BOUILLANCOURT for the purpose of preparing winter billets.	
"	21.10.16.		Notified that 643 Sergt: Corris had been appointed to a permanent commission in the South Lancs: Regt: (and seconded in M.G.Corps) from date of taking up his duties.	
"	22.10.16.		23. N.C.Os., and men arrived from Base. Notified that 2nd Lieut L.G.L.Peacocke and 2nd Lieut: R.I.Ward, had been posted to K.D.Gds., from Special Reserve and to rank with seniority as from 4.9.16.	

Army Form C. 2118.

WAR DIARY
or
INTELLIGENCE SUMMARY

(*Erase heading not required.*)

Place	Date	Hour	Summary of Events and Information	Remarks and references to Appendices
MACHY	22.10.16.		Notified that S.S.M.Percival who proceeded to 33rd Brigade Hqtrs: on 15.8.16. and was given a 2nd: Lieutantency in the 7th Battn: Norfolk Regt: and not the Border Regt: as previously stated.	
"	23.10.16.		Notified that 9881 Pte: Dinsdale B. Sqdn: died of wounds on 26.9.16. received in action at Trones Wood. while publishing at Gueudecourt	
"	25.10.16.		12. men were sent to BOISMONT to assist the R.E's., in unloading material in connection with winter billets.	
"	27.10.16.		4. R.Horses and 2 pack mules arrived from Base.	
"	28.10.16.		2nd Lieut: W.J.P.Dicks, 2nd Lieut F.H.K.Barraclough and 40 N.C.Os and men proceeded to COIGNEUX area to form a Divisional working party.	
"	29.10.16.		Notified that Lieut A.B.Richardson had been evacuated from hospital to England per hospital ship on 18.10.16.	
"	30.10.16.		The billeting party which left on 20th inst returned owing to the postponement of the move.	

Lieut-Colonel.
Comdg: 1st King's Dragoon Guards.

Army Form C. 2118.

WAR DIARY
or
INTELLIGENCE SUMMARY
(Erase heading not required.)

Instructions regarding War Diaries and Intelligence Summaries are contained in F. S. Regs., Part II. and the Staff Manual respectively. Title Pages will be prepared in manuscript.

Place	Date	Hour	Summary of Events and Information	Remarks and references to Appendices
			SUPPLEMENT TO WAR DIARY FOR OCTOBER 1916. **	
	April 24th 1916.		Pte: Shiels granted a Commission as 2nd: Lieut in 19th Battn: Lancashire Fusiliers.	
	June 12th 1916.		Corpl: Rogers granted a commission as 2nd Lieut: in the 15th Battn: Royal Warwick Regt:	
	Septr: 19th 1916.		Pte: Glen proceeded to England as a canditate for the Cadet School on being nominated for a Commission in the Fife & Forfar Yeomanry.	
			The following W.O., N.C.Os., and men have been awarded the Military Medal for conspicuous gallantry during the operations at HOOGE June 1915.	
			50864 S.S.M., W.Webb M.G.C. 50867 Sergt: W.Stratford M.G.C) Transferred from K.D.Gds: 50870 Corpl: A.H.Bramley M.G.C) 6026 Pte: J.Habgood K.D.G. 3716 " J.Hill K.D.G.	

Army Form C. 2118.

WAR DIARY or INTELLIGENCE SUMMARY.

1st K.D. Guards

(Erase heading not required.)

Instructions regarding War Diaries and Intelligence Summaries are contained in F.S. Regs., Part II. and the Staff Manual respectively. Title pages will be prepared in manuscript.

Place	Date	Hour	Summary of Events and Information	Remarks and references to Appendices
MIANNAY	1.11.16.		4 Men and 2 Trumpeters arrived from the Base.	
MIANNAY	2.11.16.		The Regiment paraded at 8.0.a.m. and marched via MOUVION - SAILLY LE SEC - PORT LE GRAND and GOUY to a new billeting area at MIANNAY, arriving at 11.45.a.m. Sqdns: went into billets as follows:- A & B Sqdns: & R.H.Q. MIANNAY. C Sqdn: BOUILLANCOURT. D Sqdn: LAMBERCOURT. A Echelon marched in rear of the Regiment. B Echelon, under 2nd Lieut: J.P.Moreton paraded at 7.30.a.m. and marching by the same route as the Regiment, arrived at 12.30.p.m. 2. Notified that 3417 Pte: Wells A Sqdn, and 3763 Pte: Rogers A Sqdn: who were with the working party attached to XIII Corps, had been wounded on 31.10.16.	
MIANNAY	3.11.16.		Notified that Major R.S.HUNT had been appointed Tempy: Lieut: Colonel, to command 8th Battn: Kings Own Royal Lancs: Regt:	
MIANNAY	8.11.16.		10 Men arrived from the Base.	
MIANNAY	10.11.16.		2nd Lieut: W.LANGFORD and 6163 Sgt: STOCK C Sqdn: proceeded to CAYEUX to take up the appointments of Tempy: Capt: & Adjt: and Q.M.S. respectively, at the Divnl: School which was to be opened on 17th inst:	
MIANNAY	12.11.16.		7 Men proceeded to the Divnl: School, completing a staff of 1 Officer and 8 O.Ranks provided by the Regiment.	
MIANNAY	13.11.16.		2nd Lieut: C.Hadlow arrived from the Base.	

Army Form C. 2118.

WAR DIARY
or
INTELLIGENCE SUMMARY.

(Erase heading not required.)

Instructions regarding War Diaries and Intelligence Summaries are contained in F. S. Regs., Part II and the Staff Manual respectively. Title pages will be prepared in manuscript.

Place	Date	Hour	Summary of Events and Information	Remarks and references to Appendices
MIANNAY	18.11.16.		A Pioneer Battalion was formed out of the Lucknow Brigade, 8 Officers and 270 O.Ranks forming part of the Battalion with Transport, paraded at 10.0.a.m. near MIANNAY for inspection by the Divisional Commander.	
MIANNAY	19.11.16.		The Divisional Commander inspected M1.O.W PIONEER BATTN: and at the same time presented ribbons of medals recently awarded to officers and O.Ranks of the Division. No:6026 L/Cpl: HABGOOD and 3716 L/Cpl: HILL had been awarded the Military Medal, but the latter being in England, through sickness, was not present at the presentation.	
MIANNAY	21.11.16.		The Pioneer Company and Hqtr: details, consisting of 8 Officers and 270 O.Ranks, paraded at the Place MIANNAY at 3.45.p.m. and proceeded by lorry to PONT REMY, the entraining point for the Lucknow Battn: The transport, consisting of 4 G.S.limbered wagons, 1 G.S. wagon 1 Medical cart and 1 water cart, paraded under S.S.M. Browning, at the Place MIANNAY at 1.30.p.m. and proceeded by road to the PONT REMY. The Battalion entrained at about 10.0.p.m. Much difficulty was experienced with the transport, owing to the railway trucks being high above the level of the siding, and the wagons, laden, had to be got on to the trucks by manual labour. The men were accommodated in the horse boxes.	
	22.11.16.		The Battalion detrained at MERICOURT about 3.30.p.m. and marched off at 5.30.a.m. arriving at FRICOURT, 3 miles distant at about 9.0.a.m.	
	23.11.16.		The remainder of the day was spent in improving the camp. The Company paraded at 7.20.a.m., proceeded to the R.E. dump, and commenced work in preparing trenches for the laying of water pipes to the front line.	

Army Form C. 2118.

WAR DIARY
or
INTELLIGENCE SUMMARY.

(Erase heading not required.)

Place	Date	Hour	Summary of Events and Information	Remarks and references to Appendices
MIANNAY	26/11/16		2nd Lieut. F.K. MURRAY JOHN SPU volunteers to Hospital	
MI ANNAY	27.11.16		2nd Lieut. H.L.Walter arrived from the Base and posted to A Sqdn:	
MI ANNAY	29.11.16		Major R.S.Spurrier left for England to be attached to 1st Reserve Regiment for 2 or 3 months.	

W.H.Cooper Capt & adjutant
King's Dragoon Guards

Army Form C. 2118.

WAR DIARY
or
INTELLIGENCE SUMMARY.
(Erase heading not required.)

Place	Date	Hour	Summary of Events and Information	Remarks and references to Appendices
			Supplement to War Diary for November 1916.	

    List of Medals Awarded.

  Long Service and Good Conduct.
    No:4055 Sgt: Franklin. 1st K.D.Gds:

  Distinguished Conduct Med.l.
    2nd Lieut: E.Percival. 7th Batn: Norfolk Regt:
           (late K.D.Gds;)

  Military Cross.
    2nd Lieut: R.Alford. Loyal North Lancs: Regt:
           (late K.D.Gds)

  Meritorious Service Medal.
    7265 Far: Sgt: Ford. 1st K.D.Gds:
        attached to Vety: Services.
    5364 Sgt: Durden. 1st K.D.Gds:
        Attached Anbala Bde: Hqtrs:

    ****

SERIAL NO. 71

Confidential
War Diary
of
1st King's Dragoon Guards.

FROM 1st December 1916. TO 31st December 1916.

Army Form C. 2118.

WAR DIARY
or
INTELLIGENCE SUMMARY
(Erase heading not required.)

Instructions regarding War Diaries and Intelligence Summaries are contained in F. S. Regs., Part II. and the Staff Manual respectively. Title Pages will be prepared in manuscript.

Place	Date	Hour	Summary of Events and Information	Remarks and references to Appendices
MIANNAY,	1.1.12.16.		At 2.30 a.m. the Germans commenced shelling the Camp of the Pioneer Battn: A shell burst between 2 tents causing the death of 6710 Tptr. Oxford and 3598 Pte. McKenzie, and wounding 10827 Pte. McBride, and 7881 L/Cpl. Cotterell, the latter was only slightly wounded and was able to remain at his duty. The 2 men who were killed were buried at LONGUEVAL ALLEY, and crosses were erected over the graves. 2nd Lieut. B.G.Holt rejoined from Lucknow M.Gun Sqdn: and posted to A Sqdn: 2nd Lieut. F.K.Murray Johnson discharged from hospital and resumed his course of instruction at Divnl: Signal Sqdn.	
MIANNAY,	3.12.16.		5 Signallers arrived from the Base.	
MIANNAY,	4.12.16.		Lieut-Colonel H.F.Wickham rejoined from Pioneer Battn: 2nd Lieut. L.G.L.Peacocke evacuated to hospital from Pioneer Battn:	
MIANNAY,	6.12.16.		2nd Lieut. W.S.H.Parker arrived from Base and posted to D Sqdn.	
MIANNAY,	8.12.16.		8 Reinforcements arrived from the Base.	
MIANNAY,	10.12.16.		2nd Lieut. J.A.Bogle-Smith arrived from the Base and posted to B Sqdn. 2 Reinforcements arrived from the Base. Capt. L.W.Alexander rejoined from Lucknow Pioneer Battn.	
MIANNAY,	13.12.16.		2nd Lieut. H.L.Walter, 2ndLieut. J.G.E.Tiarks, Lieut. W.H.Muir, 2nd Lieut. F.H.K.Barraclough and 109 N.C.O's and men paraded at the PLACE, MIANNAY, at 4.45 p.m. and proceeded to PONT REMY Railway Station, in lorries. The party entrained at this point and proceeded to FRICOURT to relieve some of the personnel of the Pioneer Battn.	
MIANNAY,	14.12.16.		2nd Lieut. J.P.Dicks, 2nd Lieut. C.Hadlow, 2nd Lieut. J.P.Brewer and 92 N.C.O's and men rejoined from Pioneer Battn.	

2449 Wt. W14957/M90 750,000 1/16 J.B.C. & A. Forms/C.2118/12.

Army Form C. 2118.

WAR DIARY
or
INTELLIGENCE SUMMARY

(Erase heading not required.)

Instructions regarding War Diaries and Intelligence Summaries are contained in F. S. Regs., Part II. and the Staff Manual respectively. Title Pages will be prepared in manuscript.

Place	Date	Hour	Summary of Events and Information	Remarks and references to Appendices
MI ANNAY,	16.12.16.		Lieut. & Qr.Mr. E.R.Holt, Surrey Yeomanry, attached to Regiment as Qr.Mr. Capt. T.H.Holroyd, R.A.M.C., rejoined from Pioneer Battn.	
MI ANNAY,	18.12.16.		2nd Lieut. A.Brown rejoined from Pioneer Battn.	
MI ANNAY,	21.12.16.		2nd Lieut. W.Langford appointed Temporary Capt. & Adjt., 4th Cavalry Divnl: School.	
MI ANNAY,	22.12.16.		Capt. W.R.F.Cooper proceeded to Lucknow Pioneer Battn: to relieve Capt. E.A.Wienholt, in command of K.D.G. Company.	
MI ANNAY,	24.12.16.		5 Reinforcements arrived from the Base.	
MI ANNAY,	25.12.16.		Capt. E.A.Wienholt rejoined from Pioneer Battn.	
MI ANNAY,	28.12.16.		An enemy shell burst in the centre of the digging party of the Pioneer Battn killing 443 Cpl. Letham, wounding 8697 Pte. Livingstone, and causing 6716 Pte. Gillespie shell shock.	
MI ANNAY,	31.12.16.		Lieut. T.H.Gladstone proceeded to Pioneer Battn: to relieve Capt. Wright 29th Lancers, officiating as Adjutant.	
			Supplement to War Diary for December, 1916.	
			MEDALS. The following N.C.O's and men of L.M.Gun Sqdn: (late K.D.Gds.) awarded the MILITARY MEDAL for gallantry in the Field. 50868 Sergt. Corley. 6337 Pte. Vence. 52392 Pte. McIntosh.	

WAR DIARY
or
INTELLIGENCE SUMMARY
(Erase heading not required.)

Army Form C. 2118.

Place	Date	Hour	Summary of Events and Information	Remarks and references to Appendices
			Tempy: Capt: L.Farthing, 2nd East Lancs Regt: (late K.D.Gds.) awarded the MILITARY CROSS for conspicuous gallantry in the attack carried out by his Battn: on 23.10.16. In this attack, his Company Commander was seriously wounded, and although wounded in the nose himself, Capt. Farthing took command of the Company, and carried out his duties as Company Commander successfully. On 16th November, whilst in the support trench, Capt. Farthing was killed by a shell. He was buried just behind the trenches, it being impossible to get him to the rear.	

for Lieut-Colonel.

Commdg: 1st King's Dragoon Guards.

www.ingramcontent.com/pod-product-compliance
Lightning Source LLC
Chambersburg PA
CBHW081551160426

43191CB00011B/1899